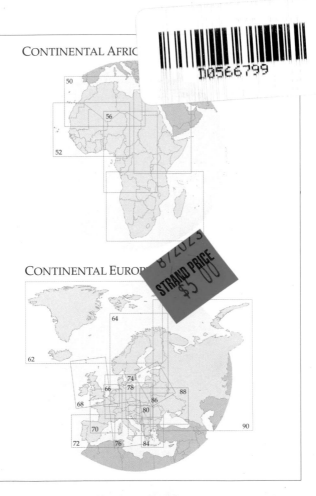

CONTINENTAL AFRICA

CONTINENTAL EUROPE

D0566799

DORLING KINDERSLEY
ULTIMATE POCKET

WORLD
ATLAS

PROJECT CARTOGRAPHY AND DESIGN
Julia Lunn   Peter Winfield

CARTOGRAPHIC RESEARCH
Michael Martin

PROJECT EDITOR AND INDEX-GAZETTEER
Jayne Parsons

DIGITAL BASE MAPS PRODUCED ON DK CARTOPIA BY
Simon Lewis   Rob Stokes   Thomas Robertshaw

PRODUCTION CONTROLLER
Hilary Stephens

EDITORIAL DIRECTOR
Andrew Heritage

ART DIRECTOR
Chez Picthall

A DK PUBLISHING BOOK
First American Edition, 1996
2 4 6 8 10 9 7 5 3 1

Published in the United States by DK Publishing, Inc.,
95 Madison Avenue, New York, New York 10016

A CIP catalog record for this book is available from the Library of Congress

ISBN: 0-7894-0192-4

Film output in England by Euroscan
Printed and bound in Italy by L.E.G.O

DORLING KINDERSLEY
ULTIMATE POCKET
WORLD
ATLAS

Key

— —	International border
– –	Disputed border
– –	Claimed border
~	International border along river
~	State border
~	State border along river
~	River
~	Lake
~	Canal
~	Seasonal river
~	Seasonal lake
—↓—	Waterfall
—	Road
—	Railway
●	Capital city
◎	Major town
○	Minor town
●	Major port
•	Minor port
✈	International airport
▲	Spot height – feet
•	Spot depth – feet

Contents

THE PHYSICAL WORLD

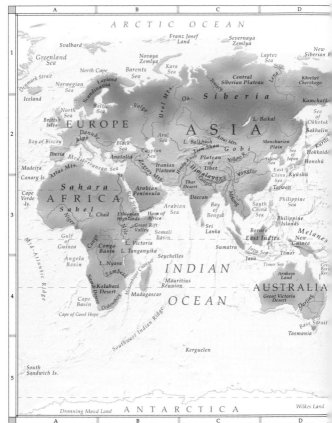

ARCTIC OCEAN

Svalbard
Franz Josef Land
Severnaya Zemlya
New Siberian Is

Greenland Sea
Novaya Zemlya
Laptev Sea

North Cape
Barents Sea
Kara Sea
Khrebet Cherskogo

Norwegian Sea
Lapland
Scandinavia
Central Siberian Plateau
Lena

Iceland
North Sea
Baltic Sea
Ob'
Siberia
Kamchatka

Denmark Strait

British Isles
EUROPE
Volga
Ural Mts.
ASIA
L. Baikal
Sea of Okhotsk

Bay of Biscay
Alps
Danube
Black Sea
Aral Sea
L. Balkhash
Altai Mts.
Gobi
Sakhalin

Iberia
Mediterranean Sea
Caspian Sea
Tien Shan
Manchurian Plain
Kurile Is

Madeira
Atlas Mts.
Anatolia
Zagros Mts.
Iranian Plateau
Hindu Kush
Plateau of Tibet
Yellow R.
Sea of Japan
Hokkaidō
Honshū

Canary Is.
Himalayas
Yangtze
East China Sea
Kyūshū

Cape Verde Is.
Sahara
AFRICA
Arabian Peninsula
Thar Desert
Ganges
Taiwan

Sahel
L. Chad
Niger
Ethiopian Highlands
Horn of Africa
Arabian Sea
Deccan
Bay of Bengal
Mekong
South China Sea
Philippine Islands

Gulf of Guinea
Nile
Great Rift Valley
Somali Basin
Sri Lanka
Borneo
East Indies
Melanes
New Guinea

Congo Basin
L. Victoria
L. Tanganyika
Seychelles
Sumatra
Java Sea
Java
Timor
Timor Sea
Gre Barri Ree

Angola Basin
L. Nyasa
Zambezi
Arnhem Land

Mid-Atlantic Ridge
Namib Desert
Mozambique Channel
INDIAN
Mauritius
Réunion
AUSTRALIA
Great Victoria Desert
Darling

Kalahari Desert
Madagascar
OCEAN
Bass Strait

Cape Basin
Cape of Good Hope
Drakensberg
Tasmania

Southwest Indian Ridge
Kerguelen

South Sandwich Is.

Dronning Maud Land
ANTARCTICA
Wilkes Land

THE POLITICAL WORLD

For full list of abbreviations see page 134.

	E		F		G		H	

O C E A N

Queen Elizabeth Is.

Greenland
(Denmark)

Victoria I.   Baffin I.

ALASKA
(USA)

C A N A D A   A T L A N T I C

Aleutian Is. (USA)

P A C I F I C
O C E A N

UNITED STATES
OF AMERICA

Bermuda
(U.K.)

Puerto Rico
(USA)
Virgin Is.
(USA)   British Virgin Is.
(U.K.)   Anguilla
(U.K.)

DOMINICAN REP.

BAHAMAS   Turks &
Caicos Is.   ANTIGUA &
BARBUDA
(U.K.)

CUBA   Guadeloupe
(France)

Cayman Is.   HAITI   DOMINICA
Martinique
(France)

JAMAICA   ST KITTS & NEVIS   ST LUCIA   BARBADOS
Montserrat
(U.K.)   ST LUCIA   GRENADA
Aruba   ST VINCENT
Netherlands Antilles   & THE GRENADINES
(Neth.)   TRINIDAD & TOBAGO

Hawaii
(USA)

MARSHALL IS.

MEXICO   BELIZE
GUATEMALA   HONDURAS
EL SALVADOR   NICARAGUA
COSTA RICA
PANAMA

NAURU

TUVALU

KIRIBATI

Wallis & Futuna
(France)

Tokelau Cook Is.
(N.Z.)   (N.Z.)
American
Samoa
(USA)
Niue
(N.Z.)

French Polynesia
(France)

COLOMBIA   French
Guiana
(France)

ECUADOR   GUYANA
SURINAME

PERU   B R A Z I L

FIJI

VANUATU
SOLOMON IS.
New Caledonia
(France)

TONGA
WESTERN
SAMOA

Pitcairn Is.
(U.K.)

PARAGUAY   BOLIVIA

NEW ZEALAND

P A C I F I C
O C E A N

CHILE   URUGUAY
ARGENTINA

A T L A N T I C
O C E A N

Falkland Is.
(U.K.)   South Georgia
(U.K.)

South
Sandwich Is.
(U.K.)

South Shetland Is.
(U.K.)   South Orkney Is.
(U.K.)

	E		F		G		H	

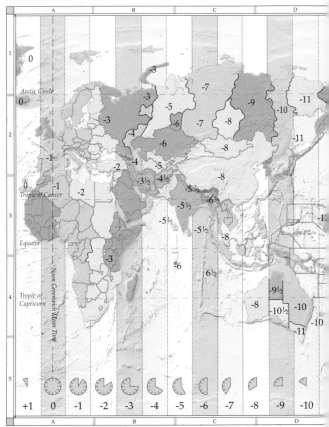

Numbers on the map indicate the number of hours which must be added or subtracted, as appropriate, in that time zone to reach GMT.

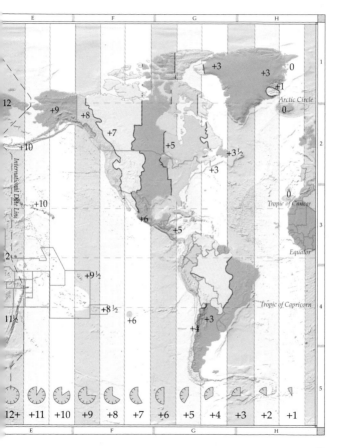

THE ARCTIC OCEAN

ASIA

Tiksi

Lena

Laptev Sea

East Siberian Sea

New Siberian Is. (Russ. Fed.)

Severnaya Zemlya

Lomonosov (Harris) Ridge

Pevek

Wrangel I. (Russ. Fed.)

Arctic Circle

Chukchi Sea

Bering Strait

Limit of permanent pack ice

ARCTIC OCEAN

Fram (Amundsen) Basin

Canada (Laurentian) Basin

NORTH AMERICA

Mackenzie

Tuktoyaktuk

Beaufort Sea

Banks's I. (Canada)

Melville I. (Canada)

Prince Patrick I. (Canada)

Bathurst I. (Canada)

Queen Elizabeth Is. (Canada)

0 km   500

0 miles   500

CONTINENTAL NORTH AMERICA

ARCTIC OCEAN

Limit of permanent pack-ice

Chukchi
Sea

Melville I.

Viscount Melville Sound

Banks I.

Beaufort
Sea

Amundsen Gulf

Victoria I.

Brooks Range ▲ 9,059ft

Arctic Circle

ASIA

Bering Strait

USA
(Alaska)

Denali
20,333ft

▲ Mackenzie

Great
Bear Lake

St Lawrence I.

Yukon

Alaska Range

Mt. Logan
19,850ft

Rocky Mountains

Great
Slave Lake

C A N

Nunivak I.

Bering
Sea

Alaska
Peninsula

Kodiak I.

Queen
Charlotte Is.

N

Great

Aleutian Islands

Queen Charlotte
Sound

Gulf
of
Alaska

U

Aleutian Trench

Vancouver I.
Mt. Rainier
14,410ft
Mt. St Helens
8,366ft

Coast Ranges

Cascade Range

Great
Basin

Great
Salt Lake

Black
Hills

Rio Grande

PACIFIC

Mt. Whitney
14,491ft

Death
Valley
-282ft

Colorado
Plateau

OCEAN

Sonoran
Desert

Sierra Madre
Occidental

Gulf of
California

Tropic of Cancer

Baja
California

USA
Hawaiian Is.

Colima
14,206ft

0 km   1000

0 miles   1000

E F G H

1

Axel
Heiberg I.
Ellesmere I.
Knud Rasmussen Land
Queen Elizabeth Is.
Devon I.
Lancaster Sound
Prince of Somerset I.
Wales I.
Baffin I.
Baffin Bay
Greenland
(Denmark)

Gunnbjørn Field▲
12,139ft
Arctic Circle

Southampton I.
Davis Strait
Denmark Strait
Iceland

Hudson Strait
EUROPE
(60)))

2

Reindeer
Lake
Hudson
Bay
Ungava
Peninsula
Ungava
Bay
Labrador
Sea
A D A
Belcher Is.
James
Bay
Labrador
L. Winnipeg
Labrador Basin

A
L. Superior
Laurentian Plateau
Strait of Belle Isle
Newfoundland
Great Lakes
Gulf of
St. Lawrence
St Pierre
& Miquelon
(France)
C. Race

3

s
Missouri
L. Huron
L. Ontario
Niagara
Falls
Grand
Banks
L. Michigan
L. Erie
Platte
Ohio
6,683ft▲
Cape Cod

Arkansas
Red R.
Mississippi
Appalachian Mts.
Sohm Plain
Azores
(Portugal)

P l a i n s
Cape
Hatteras
Bermuda
(UK)
A T L A N T I C
(46)))

4

Mississippi
Delta
The
Everglades
Nares Plain
O C E A N
MEXICO
Gulf
of
Mexico
Straits of Florida
Tropic of Cancer

▲Citlaltépetl
18,701ft
BAHAMAS
Turks & Caicos Is. (UK)
Citlaltépetl
18,701ft
CUBA
DOMINICAN REP.
Puerto Rico (USA)
Cayman Is.
(UK)
British Virgin Is. (UK)
Anguilla (UK)
ANTIGUA & BARBUDA
BELIZE
JAMAICA
HAITI
(USA) Virgin Is.
Montserrat (UK)
Guadeloupe (France)
ST KITTS & NEVIS
DOMINICA
GUATEMALA
HONDURAS
Aruba
(Neth.)
ST LUCIA
Martinique (France)
(48)))
EL SALVADOR
Caribbean
ST VINCENT &
BARBADOS
NICARAGUA
Sea
GRENADA
THE GRENADINES
Neth. Antilles
(Neth.)
TRINIDAD
& TOBAGO
COSTA RICA
PANAMA
(36)))
SOUTH AMERICA

5

E F G H

WESTERN CANADA & ALASKA

RUSSIAN FEDERATION

Wrangel I.

ARCT

OCEA

Attu I.

Bering Sea

Bering Strait

Kiska I.

St. Lawrence I.

Prudho Bay

Brooks Range

Aleutian Islands

Nunivak I.

Yukon

ALASKA (USA)

Fairbanks

Umnak I.

Dutch Harbor

Unalaska I.

Alaska Range

Aleutian Trench

Anchorage

Dawso

Kodiak I.

Kodiak

Valdez

Cordova

YUKON TERRITOR

WHITEHORSE

Gulf of Alaska

JUNEAU

PACIFIC

Ketchikan

OCEAN

Prince Rupert

Queen Charlotte Is.

Queen Charlotte Sound

Port Alice

Vancouver I.

VICTOR

0 km   400

0 miles   400

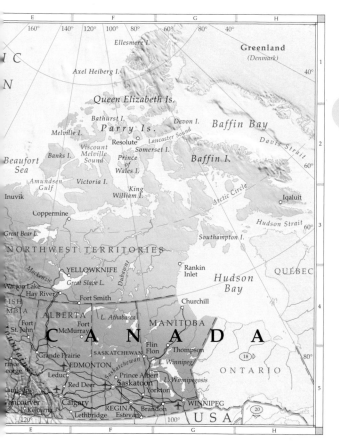

EASTERN CANADA

0 km 400

0 miles 400

70°   60°   12   50°   60°

Baffin I.

Hudson Strait   Labrador
Akpatok I.   Sea
(NW Territories)   C. Chidley
                                    Labrador Basin
Ungava
Bay   46

Kuujjuaq   Nain   ATLANTIC

                          Hopedale   OCEAN
Schefferville   Makkovik
                   Labrador   Cartwright
         Smallwood
         Reservoir   Port Hope Simpson
Réservoir   Churchill Falls Happy Valley-   Strait of Belle Isle
Caniapiscau   Goose Bay
Labrador City   50°

D   A   Havre-   Newfoundland
     Réservoir   Saint-Pierre   Gander
     Manicouagan   Grand Falls   Clarenville
E C   Sept-Îles   Île d'Anticosti   ST JOHN'S
                                        Corner Brook
     L. Saint-Jean   St. Lawrence Gulf of St. Lawrence Channel-Port-aux-Basques C. Race
Jonquière   Gaspé   St Pierre
Chicoutimi   St Pierre & Miquelon
         Bathurst PRINCE   (France)   Grand Banks
QUÉBEC   NEW   EDWARD
     FREDERICTON BRUNSWICK ISLAND CHARLOTTETOWN
Trois-Rivières   Moncton Sydney
Sherbrooke MAINE   20   NOVA SCOTIA
Montréal   Saint John   Dartmouth
NEW   HALIFAX
HAMPSHIRE   Yarmouth
                        C. Sable   Sohm Plain
VERMONT
MASSACHUSETTS   ATLANTIC
     RHODE ISLAND
CONNECTICUT 70°   OCEAN   60°

E   F   G

19

USA: THE NORTHEAST

0 km   200

0 miles   200

USA: CENTRAL STATES

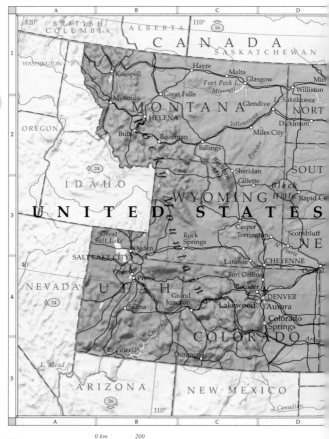

0 km   200

0 miles   200

USA: THE WEST

0 km   200

0 miles   200

USA: THE SOUTHWEST

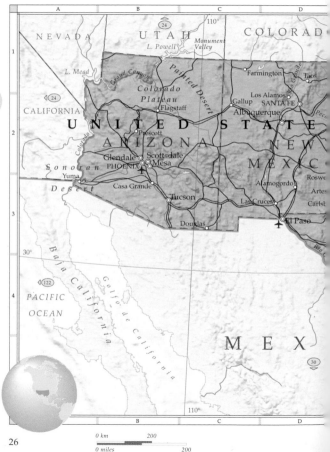

0 km   200

0 miles   200

USA: THE SOUTHEAST

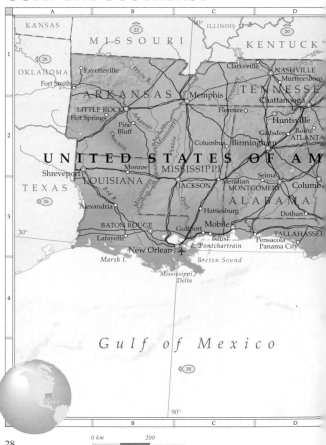

0 km   200

0 miles   200

MEXICO

MEXICO

STATES OF AMERICA
LOUISIANA

T E X A S

Rio Grande
Nuevo Laredo
Monclova
Reynosa
Monterrey
Matamoros
Saltillo

Ciudad Victoria

O
r
i
e
n
t
a
l

San Luis Potosí
Tampico
Pánuco

León
Irapuato
Querétaro
Pachuca
Poza Rica

Morelia
MEXICO
CITY
Jalapa
Cuernavaca
Puebla
Veracruz
Uruapan
Balsas
Sierra Madre del Sur
Oaxaca

Acapulco

America Trench

100°

Gulf

of

Mexico

Tropic of Cancer

Bahía de Campeche

Coatzacoalcos
Minatitlán
Villahermosa

Tuxtla
Gutiérrez

Golfo
de
Tehuantepec
Tapachula

Cancún
Mérida
L. de
Cozumel
Campeche
Yucatan
Peninsula

BELIZE

GUATEMALA

90°

34

32

31

CENTRAL AMERICA

M E X I C O

Usumacinta

90°

Belize City
BELMOPAN
Flores   San Ignacio
BELIZE

Islas de la Bahía

GUATEMALA

Huehuetenango   Cobán   *Lago de Izabal*   Puerto   Puerto Cortés   Trujillo
                                              Barrios
Quezaltenango   Zacapa   San Pedro   La Ceiba
                                              Sula
GUATEMALA   Santa Rosa   *Gulf of Honduras*
Mazatenango   **CITY**   de Copán   Comayagua   **HONDURAS**   *Patuca*
                    Escuintla   La Esperanza   Juticalpa
                                                              TEGUCIGALPA   *Coco*
                              Santa Ana
SAN SALVADOR   San Miguel
      EL SALVADOR   San Lorenzo   Somoto
                                    Choluteca   Jinotega
                            Gulf of Fonseca   Estelí   Matagalpa   **NICARAGUA**
                              Chichigalpa
                              Corinto   León
                                    MANAGUA   Juigalpa
Middle America Trench   Granada   *Lago de*
                                          Nicaragua   *Río San Juan*
                                    Rivas

P A C I F I C   *Península de*   Liberia
                                   Nicoya
10°   Puntarenas   Alajuel
                                          SAN JOSÉ

O C E A N

                                          Golfo de Nicoya

90°

0 km   200

0 miles   200

Cayman Trench

Islas Santanilla
(Honduras)

JAMAICA

Greater Antilles

HAITI

Bajo Nuevo
(Colombia)

34

Caribbean

Cayos Miskitos
(Nicaragua)

I. de Providencia
(Colombia)

Sea

I. de San Andrés
(Colombia)

Islas del Maiz (Nicaragua)

Mosquito Coast

Bluefields

COSTA
RICA

Limón

Cartago

PANAMA

Colón

PANAMA CITY

Gulf
of
Darien

Penonomé

Panama
Canal

David

Santiago

Golfo
de
Chiriquí

Chitré
Las Tablas

Isla del
Rey

Golfo
de
Panamá

COLOMBIA

38

80°

THE CARIBBEAN

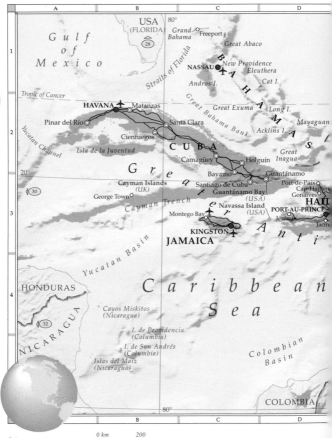

0 km   200

0 miles   200

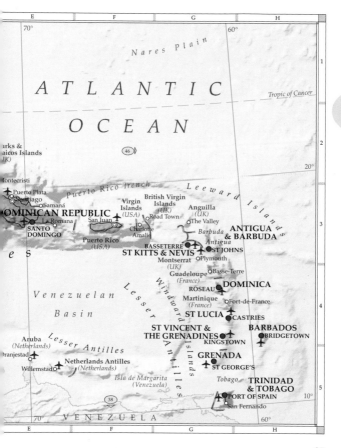

CONTINENTAL SOUTH AMERICA

CENTRAL
AMERICA

Middle America Trench

Caribbean Sea

Lesser Antilles

Greater Antilles

Gulf of Darien

VENEZUELA

COLOMBIA

Trinidad

Netherlands Antilles

French Guiana (France)

SURINAME

GUYANA

Angel Falls

Guiana Highlands

Apure

Rio Negro

Japurá

Caquetá

ECUADOR

Galápagos Is. (Ecuador)

Equator

Chimborazo 20,562ft

Cotopaxi 19,347ft

Ruiz 17,717ft

19,029ft

Marañón

Ucayali

Huascarán 22,206ft

PERU

Madeira

Amazon

A m a z o n i a

Purus

BRAZIL

Amazon Delta

Ilha de Marajó

Tapajós

Xingu

Tocantins

Planalto do Mato Grosso

Araguaia

BOLLIVIA

Pantanal

PARAG

G r a n C h a c o

Paraguay

São Francisco

B r a z i l i a n H i g h l a n d s

9,144ft Mar

Represa de Sobradinho

Cabo de São Roque

Ilha Fernando de Noronha (Brazil)

ATLANTIC

OCEAN

Mid-Atlantic Ridge

46

ATLANTIC OCEAN

Equator

14

Gulf of Guayaquil

PACIFIC
OCEAN

Peru-Chile Trench

123

A n d e s

Tropic of Capricorn

0 km   1000

0 miles   1000

ATLANTIC

OCEAN

Argentine Basin

Chile Basin

Isla San Félix
(Chile)
Isla San Ambroso
(Chile)
Islas de los Desventurados
(Chile)

Islas Juan
Fernández
(Chile)

URUGUAY

Paraná

Río de la Plata

Laguna
dos Patos

ARGENTINA

pampas

Sierra pampas

Salado

Río del Salado

Salado

Colorado

Bahía Blanca

Golfo San Matías

Salinas Grandes

Península
Valdés
-131ft

Golfo San Jorge

Chubut

Andes

PATAGONIA

Isla
de Chiloé

Archipiélago
de los Chonos

Lago Buenos Aires

Isla Wellington

Lago
Argentino

Bahía
Grande

Río Deseado

Tierra
del Fuego

Strait of Magellan

Cape Horn

Drake Passage

Falkland Is.
(UK)

West
Falkland

East Falkland

CHILE

Mercedario
22,212ft
Aconcagua
22,826ft

Atacama

Scotia Ridge

Scotia Sea

South Orkney Is.
(UK)

South Georgia
(UK)

South
Sandwich Is.
(UK)

Limit of Permanent Pack Ice

ANTARCTICA

46

132

37

NORTHERN SOUTH AMERICA

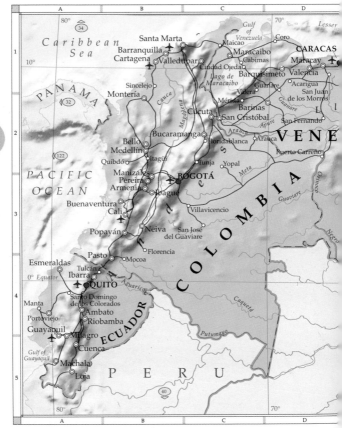

0 km   200
0 miles   200

Peru, Bolivia & North Brazil

VENEZUELA

GUYANA

COLOMBIA

Boa Vista

Guian

Rio Negro

Represa
Balbina

ECUADOR

Napo

Amazon

Manaus

Iquitos

Jurua

Amazonia

Marañón

Moyobamba

Tarapoto

BRA

P

Puru

Madeira

Pucallpa

Cruzeiro do Sul

Porto Velho

Chiclayo

Sana

Chimbote

Ucayali

Trujillo

Huaraz

Huánuco

Rio Branco

Madre de Dios

Riberalta

Piura

Huacho

La Oroya

Puerto
Maldonado

Beni

Callao

Huancayo

LIMA

Ayacucho

PERU

Cusco

Trinidad

Pisco

Ica

Nazca

Puno

BOLIVIA

Arequipa

Lake
Titicaca

LA PAZ

Cochabamba

Montero

Oruro

Punata

Santa Cruz

Tacna

Lago Poopó

Puerto Suáre

Sucre

Potosí

Puerto Busc

PARAGUA

Uyuni

Camir

CHILE

Tupiza

Tarija

Yacuiba

PACIFIC

OCEAN

Peru-Chile Trench

ARGENTINA

0 km 400

0 miles 400

SURINAME

French Guiana *(France)*

38

ATLANTIC

OCEAN

46

Highlands

Macapá

Ilha Caviana

Ilha de Marajó

Amazon

Belém

Equator 0°

Santarém

São Luís

Paranaíba

Ilha Fernando de Noronha

Xingu

Represa de Tucuruí

Imperatriz

Teresina

Fortaleza

Mossoró

Natal

es Pires

Carolina

Juàzeiro do Norte

Campina Grande

João Pessoa

Z I L

Represa de Sobradinho

São Francisco

Recife

Palmas

Juàzeiro

Maceió

10°

Araguaia

Tocantins

Aracaju

Planalto de Mato Grosso

Taguatinga

Feira de Santana

Salvador

Brazilian

Cuiabá

Anápolis

BRASÍLIA

Itabuna

Goiânia

Highlands

Vitória da Conquista

Montes Claros

Governador Valadares

Uberlândia

Abrolhos Bank

Hotspur Seamount

Uberaba

Belo Horizonte

Campo Grande

Divinópolis

Paraná

Ribeirão Preto

Vitória

20°

Marília

Nova

Campos

Campinas

Iguaçu

Juiz de Fora

Londrina

Sorocaba

Taubaté

Rio de Janeiro

42

São Paulo

Tropic of Capricorn

50°

40°

PARAGUAY, URUGUAY & SOUTH BRAZIL

0 km   200

0 miles   200

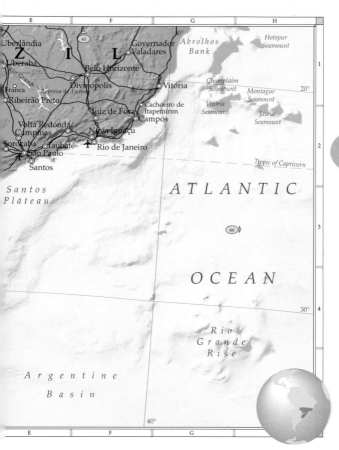

Uberlândia

Z I L

Uberaba

40

Governador
Valadares

Abrolhos
Bank

Hotspur
Seamount

Rio Grande

Belo Horizonte

França
Ribeirão Preto

Divinópolis
Represa de Furnas

Vitória

Champlain
Seamount

Montague
Seamount

20°

Juiz de Fora

Cachoeiro de
Itapemirim
Campos

Vitória
Seamount

Jaseur
Seamount

Volta Redonda
Campinas

Nova Iguaçu

Sorocaba
São Paulo

Taubaté

Rio de Janeiro

Santos

Tropic of Capricorn

*Santos
Plateau*

A T L A N T I C

46

O C E A N

30°

*Rio
Grande
Rise*

*Argentine

Basin*

40°

43

CHILE & ARGENTINA

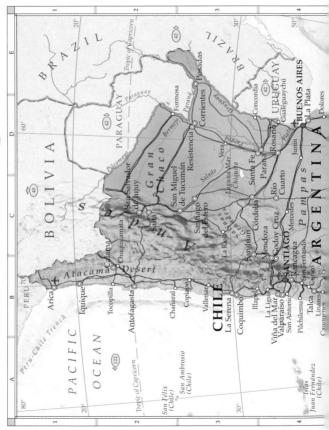

0 km   200

0 miles   200

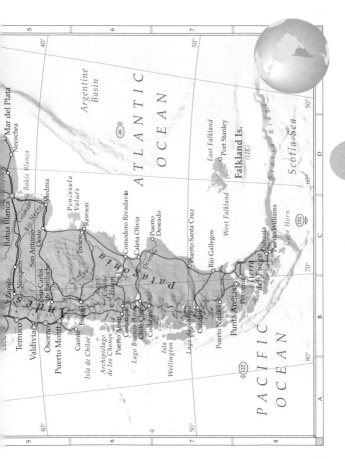

THE ATLANTIC OCEAN

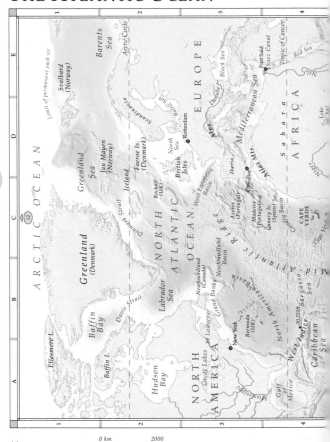

ARCTIC OCEAN

Barents Sea

Svalbard (Norway)

Limit of permanent pack ice

Arctic Circle

EUROPE

Black Sea

Port Said
Suez Canal
Red Sea
Tropic of Cancer

Greenland Sea

Scandinavia

Baltic Sea

Danube

Alps

Mediterranean Sea

Nile

Jan Mayen (Norway)

Iceland

Faeroe Is. (Denmark)

North Sea

Rotterdam

Atlas Mts.

Sahara

AFRICA

Ellesmere I.

Greenland (Denmark)

Denmark Strait

Rockall (UK)

British Isles

West European Basin

Iberia

Gibraltar

Madeira (Portugal)

Azores (Portugal)

Canary Basin

Lake Chad

Niger

NORTH ATLANTIC OCEAN

CAPE VERDE

Cape Verde

Baffin Bay

Baffin I.

Davis Strait

Labrador Sea

Newfoundland (Canada)

Newfoundland Basin

Mid-Atlantic Ridge

Hudson Bay

Great Lakes

St. Lawrence

Grand Banks

New York

Bermuda (UK)

North American Basin

30.25N

Sargasso Sea

NORTH AMERICA

Gulf of Mexico

Mississippi

West Indies

Caribbean Sea

0 km   2000

0 miles   2000

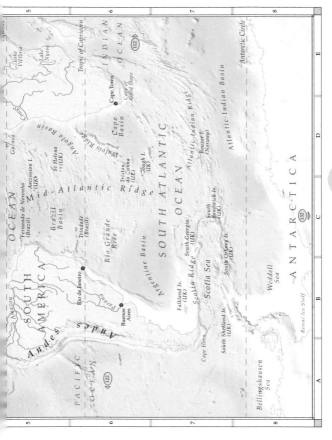

CONTINENTAL AFRICA

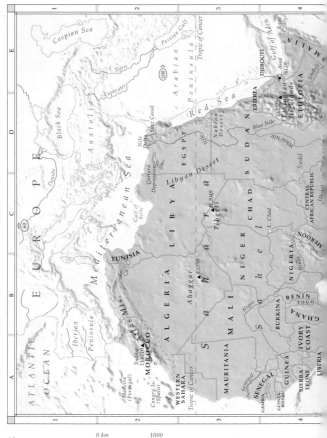

Caspian Sea

Persian Gulf

Tropic of Cancer

EUROPE

Black Sea

Tigris

Anatolia

Euphrates

Suez Canal

Arabian Peninsula

Red Sea

DJIBOUTI

Gulf of Aden

Assal -512r

SOMALIA

Egypt

ERITREA

Ethiopian Highlands

ETHIOPIA

EGYPT

Nile Delta

Nubian Desert

Blue Nile

White Nile

SUDAN

Sudd

Nile

Qattara Depression

Gulf of Sirte

Libyan Desert

LIBYA

S a h a r a

CENTRAL AFRICAN REPUBLIC

Ubangi

TUNISIA

Atlas Mts

ALGERIA

Toubkal 13,671ft

MOROCCO

Ahaggar ▲9,573ft

Tibesti ▲11,204ft

CHAD

L. Chad

NIGER

S a h e l

CAMEROON

NIGERIA

Benue

Mediterranean Sea

ATLANTIC OCEAN

Iberian Peninsula

Madeira (Portugal)

Canary Is. (Spain)

WESTERN SAHARA

Tropic of Cancer

MAURITANIA

Senegal

MALI

Niger

BURKINA

BENIN

TOGO

GHANA

IVORY COAST

LIBERIA

SIERRA LEONE

GUINEA

GUINEA BISSAU

SENEGAL

GAMBIA

0 km   1000

0 miles   1000

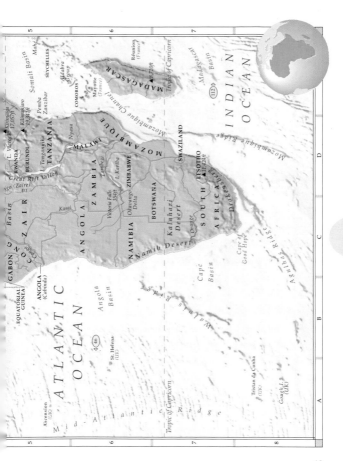

ATLANTIC OCEAN

INDIAN OCEAN

Somali Basin

SEYCHELLES

Réunion (France)

Madagascar Basin

Tropic of Capricorn

MADAGASCAR

Aldabra Group

Mayotte (France)

COMOROS

Pemba

Zanzibar

Mozambique Channel

Mozambique Ridge

Mafia

L. Victoria Kilimanjaro 19,341ft

RWANDA

Kilimanjaro 19,341ft

BURUNDI

TANZANIA

Nyasa

L. Tanganyika

MALAWI

MOZAMBIQUE

Great Rift Valley

120 (Zaire) R.

ZAMBIA

Zambezi

ZIMBABWE

L. Kariba

SWAZILAND

LESOTHO

CONGO Basin

ZAIRE

Kasai

Victoria Falls 354ft

Okavango Delta

BOTSWANA

SOUTH AFRICA

Drakensberg

GABON

Congo

ANGOLA

NAMIBIA

Kalahari Desert

Orange

Cape of Good Hope

EQUATORIAL GUINEA

ANGOLA (Cabinda)

Namib Desert

Cape Basin

Agulhas Ridge

Angola Basin

Walvis Ridge

46

St. Helena (UK)

Ascension (UK)

Tropic of Capricorn

Mid-Atlantic Ridge

Tristan da Cunha (UK)

Gough I. (UK)

112

49

NORTHWEST AFRICA

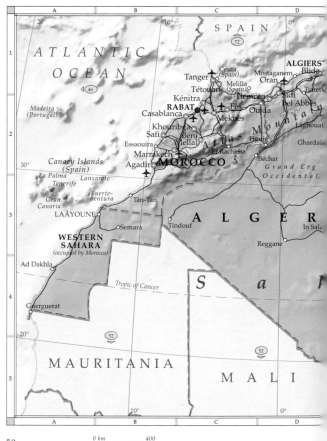

0 km 400

0 miles 400

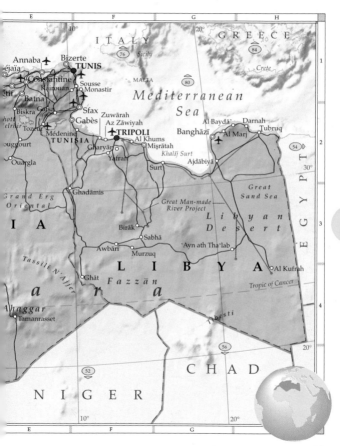

ITALY
Sicily
MALTA
GREECE
Crete
Mediterranean Sea

Annaba
éjaïa
Bizerte
TUNIS
Constantine
Kairouan
Sousse
Monastir
Batna
Biskra
Gafsa
Sfax
Zuwārah
Az Zāwiyah
Al Bayḍā'
Darnah
hott
elrhir
Tozeur
Gabès
TRIPOLI
Banghāzī
Al Marj
Tubruq
ouggourt
Médenine
TUNISIA
Al Khums
Miṣrātah
Yafran
Surt
Gharyān
Khalīj Surt
Ajdābiyā
Ouargla
Ghadāmis
Great Sand Sea
Grand Erg
Oriental
Great Man-made
River Project
L i b y a n
D e s e r t
I A
Birāk
Sabhā
'Ayn ath Tha'lab
Awbārī
Murzuq
a
Tassïle N'Ajjer
Ghāt
Fazzān
L I B Y A
Al Kufrah
Tropic of Cancer
hagar
Tamanrasset
a
r
a
Tibesti
EGYPT
CHAD
NIGER

51

0 km 250

0 miles 250

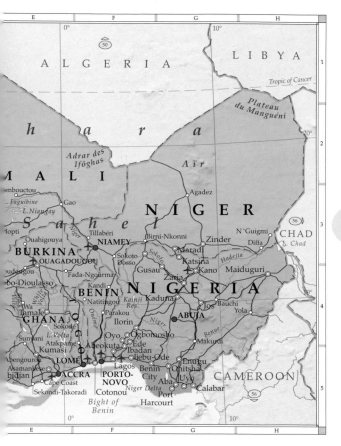

53

NORTHEAST AFRICA

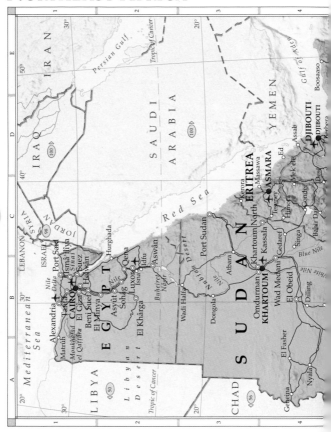

0 km   400

0 miles   400

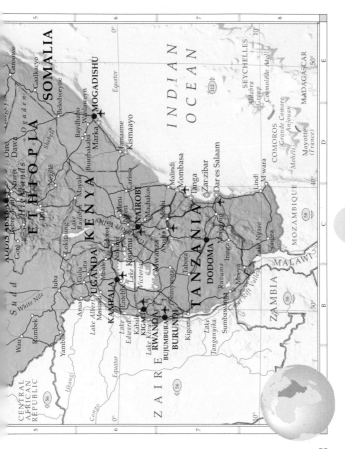

CENTRAL AFRICA

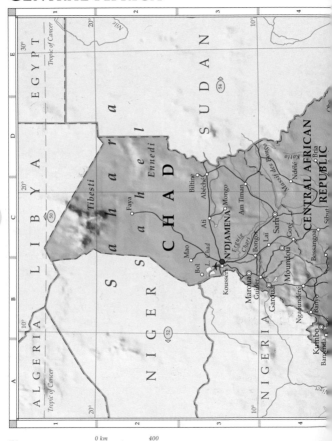

0 km 400

0 miles 400

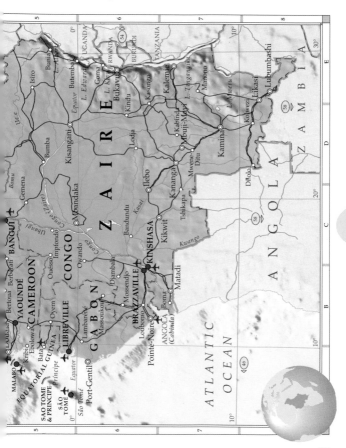

SOUTHERN AFRICA

0 km   400

0 miles   400

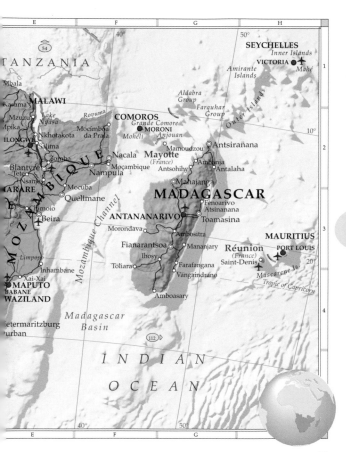

CONTINENTAL EUROPE

ARCTIC OCEAN

12

Norwegian
Basin

Arctic Circle

Norwegian
Sea

ICELAND

Faeroe-Iceland
Ridge

Faeroe Islands (Denmark)

Shetland Is.

8,100ft▲

NORWAY

Orkney Is.

SWEDE

Outer Hebrides

North
Sea

DENMARK

46

ATLANTIC

UNITED
KINGDOM

OCEAN

IRELAND

NETHERLANDS

Thames

Nort

Elbe

GERMANY

BELGIUM

LUX.

Rhine

English Channel

Seine

Danube

CZEC

FRANCE

Loire

Meuse

P

S

Biscay Plain

6,188ft▲

SWITZ.

LIECH

SLOVEN

Massif
Central

Mont Blanc

ITALY

Bay of
Biscay

Garonne

MONACO

SAN
MARINO

Adri

C. Finisterre

11,168ft▲

Pyrenees

ANDORRA

Corsica

VATICAN
CITY

PORTUGAL

SPAIN

Balearic Is.

Sardinia

Tyrrhen
Sea

Guadalquivir

Mulhacén

Etna
11,05

C. St Vincent

▲11,411ft

Mediterranean Sea

48

Sicil

Gibraltar (UK)

AFRICA

MALTA

0 km   600

0 miles   600

North Cape

Barents Sea

Lapland
6,846ft

Kola
Peninsula

Arctic Circle

White Sea

N. Dvina

Ural Mountains

FINLAND

RUSSIAN FEDERATION

Gulf of Bothnia

Gulf of Finland

92

ESTONIA

Baltic Sea

LATVIA

Dvina

Volga

LITHUANIA

RUSSIAN FED.
Kaliningrad

Plain

BELARUS

Pripet
Marshes

POLAND

uropean

Vistula

UKRAINE

Carpathians

Dnieper

Don

Volga

SLOVAKIA

HUNGARY

MOLDOVA

Sea of
Azov

Aral
Sea

ROATIA

ROMANIA

OS. &
ERZ.

YUGO

Danube

Black
Sea

Caucasus Mts.

Volga
Delta
-92ft

BULGARIA

Balkan Mts.

El'brus 18,511ft

Caspian
Sea

MAC

BANIA

Pindus
Mts.

Aegean
Sea

ASIA

onian
Sea

GREECE

Euphrates

Crete

Tigris

92

61

THE NORTH ATLANTIC

ARCTIC

Ellesmere Island
(Canada)

Lincoln
Sea

Peary Land

Independence Fjord

Nares Strait

Washington
Land

Nyeboe
Land

Knud Rasmussen Land

Kong
Frederik
VIII Land

Sermersuaq

Inglefield Land

Siorapaluk

Qaanaaq (Thule)

Pituffik

Savissivik

Greenland
(Denmark)

Kong
Christian
X Land

Mesters Vig

Baffin Bay

Kullorsuaq

Tasiusaq

Nuugaatsiaq

Umanak

Kangertittivaq

Qeqertarsuaq

Qeqertarsuaq

Ilulissat

Davis Strait

Aasiaat

Qasigiannguit

Kong Christian IX Land

Aputiteeq

Arctic Circle

Kangaatsiaq

Sisimiut

Kong
Frederik
IX
Land

Denmark

Kangerlussuaq

Ammassalik

Ísafjördhur

Baffin Island
(Canada)

Manlitsoq

Kong Frederik VI Kyst

Hafnarfjördhu

NUUK (Godthåb)

Qeqertarsuatsiaat

Paamiut

Hudson Strait

Ivittuut

Qaqortoq

Narsaq

NORTH

Nanortalik

Narsaq Kujalleq

Uummannarsuaq

Labrador Sea

ATLANTIC

CANADA

NEW-
FOUNDLAND

OCEAN

QUEBEC

0 km   500

0 miles   500

OCEAN

Wandel Sea

Greenland Sea

Svalbard
(Norway)
Nordaustlandet 80°
Spitsbergen Pyramiden
Barentsburg○ ○Longyearbyen
Edgeøya

○Danmarkshavn

Greenland Basin

○Daneborg

Mohns Ridge

Jan Mayen
(Norway)

North Cape

70°

oqqortoormiit

Norwegian Sea

Arctic Circle

○Húsavík
kureyri ○Seydhisfjördhur
REYKJAVIK ○Djúpivogur
elfoss

Faeroe Islands
(Denmark)
○Tórshavn

64

NORWAY

FINLAND

60°

ICELAND

SWEDEN

ESTONIA

Shetland (UK)

LATVIA

yville-Thomson Ridge

Orkney (UK)

Hebrides (UK)

68

DENMARK

LITH.

IRELAND
20° 10°

UNITED
KINGDOM

0°

66

NETH.

GERMANY

POLAND

10°

SCANDINAVIA & FINLAND

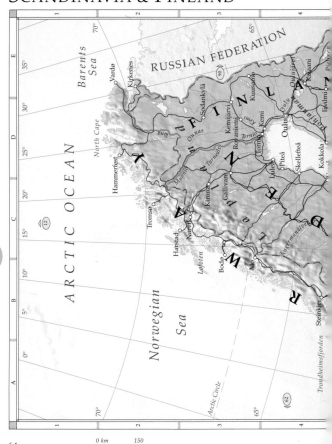

RUSSIAN FEDERATION

FINLAND

SWEDEN

Barents Sea

ARCTIC OCEAN

Norwegian Sea

Vardø
Kirkenes
North Cape
Hammerfest
Tromsø
Harstad
Narvik
Lofoten
Bodø
Mo
Steinkjer
Trondheimsfjorden

Sodankylä
Kemijärvi
Rovaniemi
Kuusamo
Kemi
Tornio
Oulu
Piteå
Skellefteå
Luleå
Kokkola
Kiruna
Gällivare
Ivalo
Inari

Arctic Circle

0° 5° 10° 15° 20° 25° 30° 35°
70° 65°

0 km   150
0 miles   150

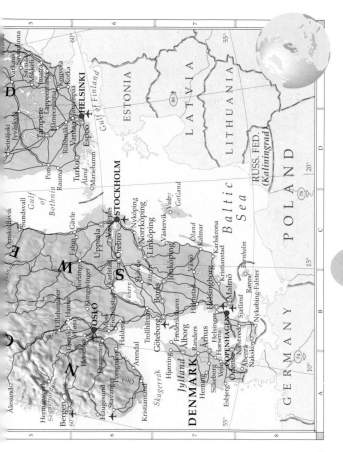

THE LOW COUNTRIES

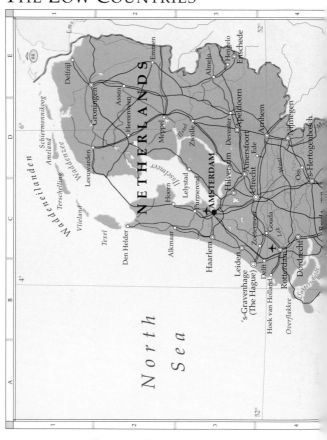

North
Sea

NETHERLANDS

Waddeneilanden
Schiermonnikoog
Ameland
Terschelling
Vlieland
Texel
Den Helder

Ems
Delfzijl
Groningen
Assen
Heerenveen
Leeuwarden

Emmen
Almelo
Hengelo
Enschede
Apeldoorn
Deventer
Arnhem
Nijmegen
Ede
Amersfoort
Utrecht
's-Hertogenbosch
Oss
Waal

Meppel
Zwolle
IJssel
IJsselmeer
Lelystad
Hilversum
AMSTERDAM
Purmerend
Hoorn

Alkmaar
Haarlem
Leiden
Zoetermeer
Gouda
Lek
Delft
's-Gravenhage
(The Hague)
Rotterdam
Dordrecht
Hoek van Holland
Overflakkee
Oosterschelde
Breda

52°
52°
6°
4°

0 km   50

0 miles   50

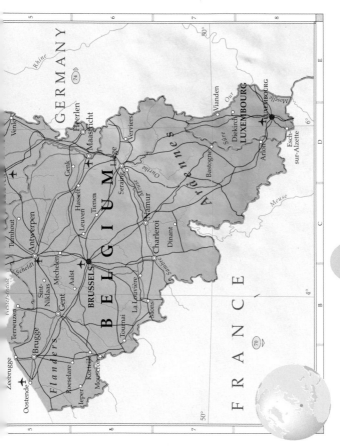

THE BRITISH ISLES

North Sea

ATLANTIC OCEAN

SCOTLAND

UNITED KINGDOM

Lerwick

Shetland

Kirkwall

Orkney

Thurso

Ullapool

Lewis

Stornoway

Outer Hebrides

North Uist

South Uist

Barra

North Minch

Little Minch

Skye

Loch Ness

Elgin

Inverness

Moray Firth

Grampian Mts

Aberdeen

Dundee

Perth

Firth of Forth

EDINBURGH

Newcastle upon Tyne

Peny

Tweed

Dumfries

Glasgow

Greenock

Mull

Oban

Loch Lomond

Jura

Arran

Ayr

Islay

Fort William

Stirling

Rosemary Bank

0 km   100

0 miles   100

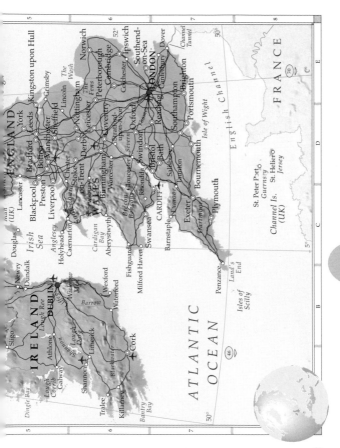

— *Administrative border*

FRANCE & ANDORRA

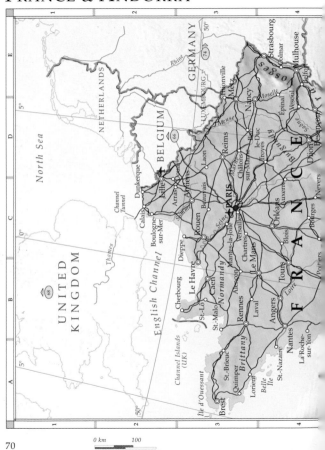

0 km   100

0 miles   100

ITALY

Genève

Annecy
Chambéry

Grenoble

45°

Lyon
St-Etienne

Roanne
St-Chamond
Le Puy

Valence

Rhône

Aix-en-
Provence

MONACO
MONTE CARLO
Nice
Côte d'Azur
Cannes

Avignon

Provence

Iles
d'Hyères

Bastia

Corse

Ligurian
Sea

Ajaccio

Sardinia
(Italy)

40°

Clermont-
Ferrand

Aurillac

Rodez

Cévennes

Nîmes

Montpellier

A-les

Marseille

Toulon

Golfe
du Lion

Massif

Central

Périgueux

Cahors

Lot

Montauban

Albi

Toulouse

Agen

Auch

Béziers

Narbonne

Perpignan

Mediterranean Sea

5°

Angoulême

Dordogne

Carcassonne

Pyrénées

ANDORRA
ANDORRA
LA VELLA

Balearic Is.
(Spain)

Bordeaux

Biscay

Garonne

Pau

Tarbes

Mont-de-Marsan

Bayonne

SPAIN

Ebro

40°

5°

6°

7°

8°

SPAIN & PORTUGAL

0 km 100

0 miles 100

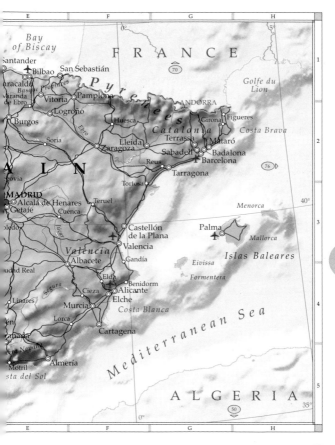

GERMANY, SWITZERLAND & AUSTRIA

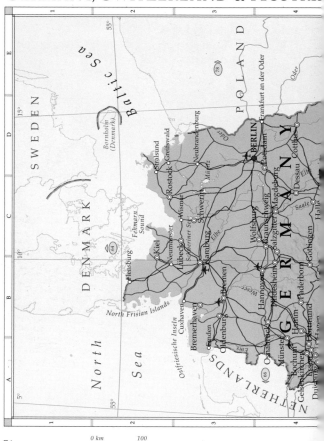

0 km   100

0 miles   100

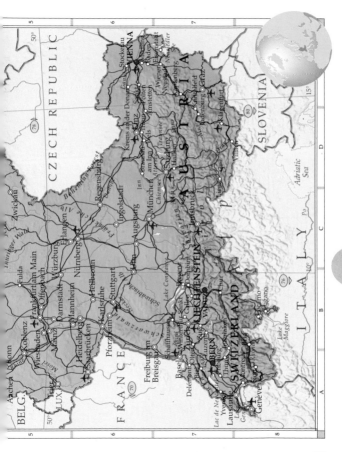

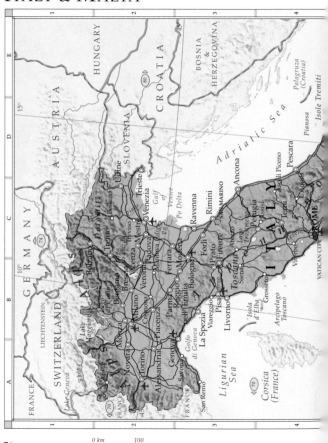

0 km 100

0 miles 100

CENTRAL EUROPE

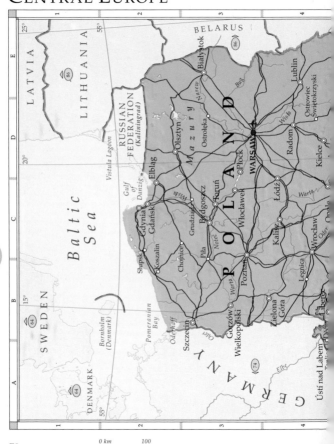

0 km   100

0 miles   100

THE WESTERN BALKANS

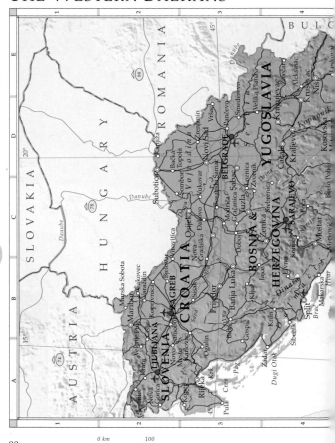

0 km   100

0 miles   100

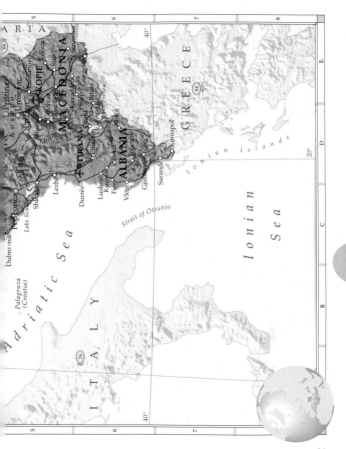

THE MEDITERRANEAN

ATLANTIC

OCEAN

English Channel

Thames

Seine

Loire

Bay
of
Biscay

Dordogne

Massif
Central

Garonne

Rhône

L. Geneva

Mt. Blanc
15,771ft

E U

Danube

Alps

Po

Apennines

9,56

C. Finisterre

Pyrenees

Halpa

Ebro

Golfe
du
Lion

Marseille

Genoa

Livorno

Corsica

Naple

Iberian

Tagus

Barcelona

Valencia

Balearic Is.

Sardinia

Tyrrheni
Sea

Peninsula

Guadalquivir

11,168ft

Gibraltar

Oran

Algiers

Tell Atlas

Tunis

Medit

Mai

C. St Vincent

Strait of Gibraltar

Rif

7,638ft

Sfax

Atlas Mountains

13,665ft

Canary Is.
(Spain)

Chott el Jerid

Grand Erg
Occidental

Grand Erg
Oriental

Tripoli

A F R I

Sahar

48

82

0 km   400

0 miles   400

BULGARIA & GREECE

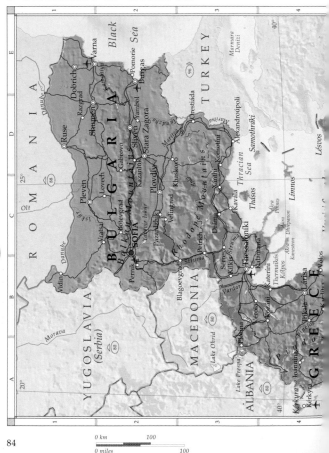

0 km   100

0 miles   100

TURKEY

Aegean Sea

Évvoia
Chalkída
ATHENS
Acharnaí
Pernaiás
Dhafni
Megára
Korinthiakós Kólpos
Dhiorigas
Korinthou
Korinthos
Trípoli

Agrínio
Lep´ádhi
Pátra

Peloponnisos

Spárti

Kalamáta

Zákynthos

Kefallinía

Lefkáda

Iónioi Nísoi

Ionian
Sea

Kýthira

Mírtoó Pelagos

Kéa
Kykládhes

Andros

Chíos

Sámos

Tínos

Páros

Mílos

Mikonos

Náxos

Íos

Ikaría

Amorgós

Thíra

Astypálaia

Dodekánisos

Kos

Ródos

Ródos

Kárpathos

Sea of Crete

Chaniá

Iráklio

Kríti

Mediterranean Sea

LIBYA

35°

25°

20°

35°

85

The Baltic States & Belarus

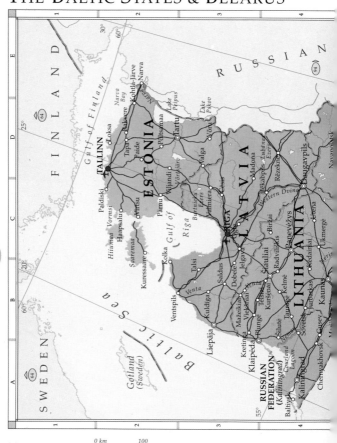

0 km 100

0 miles 100

FEDERATION

Dnieper

Vitsyebsk

Western Dvina

Orsha

Horki

Mahilyow

Byerazino

Krychaw

Byalynichy

Barysaw

Zhodzina

Babruysk

Zhlobin

Svyetlahorsk

Homyel'

Lyepyel'

Hlybokaye

Maladzyechna

BELARUS

Drisa

Rechytsa

Kalinkavichy

Mazyr

MINSK

Baranavichy

Slutsk

Salihorsk

Luninyets

Pinsk

Pripet Marshes

Pripet

Druskininkai

Hrodna

Vawkavysk

Slonim

Kobryn

Brest

Neman

Bug

POLAND

Kyyivs'ke Vdskh.

Dnieper

U K R A I N E

Dniester

Bug

88

78

50°

30°

25°

50°

40°

E

D

C

B

A

5   6   7   8

87

UKRAINE, MOLDOVA & ROMANIA

0 km   100

0 miles   100

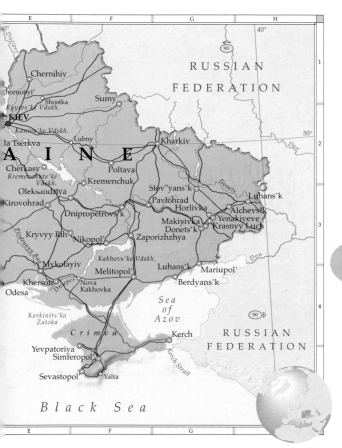

RUSSIAN

FEDERATION

Chernihiv

hornobyl'
Shostka
Kyyivs'ke Vdskh.
Sumy
KIEV
Kaniv's'ke Vdskh.
la Tserkva
Lubny
Kharkiv
A I N E
Poltava
Cherkasy
Kremenchuts'ke
Vdskh.
Kremenchuk
Slov"yans'k
Donets
Oleksandriya
Pavlohrad
Luhans'k
Kirovohrad
Horlivka
Alchevsk
Dnipropetrovsk
Makiyivka
Yenakiyeve
Donets'k
Krasnyy Luch
Kryvyy Rih
Nikopol'
Zaporizhzhya
Pivdennyy Buh
Mykolayiv
Kakhovs'ke Vdskh.
Luhans'k
Mariupol'
Kherson
Melitopol'
Berdyans'k
Nova
Odesa
Kakhovka
Dnieper
Don
Sea
of
Azov
Karkinits'ka
Zatoka
Crimea
Kerch
RUSSIAN
FEDERATION
Yevpatoriya
Simferopol'
Kerch Strait
Sevastopol'
Yalta

Black Sea

EUROPEAN RUSSIA

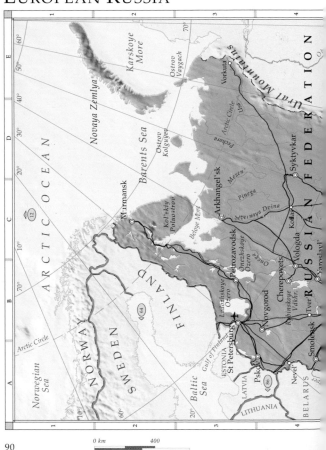

ARCTIC OCEAN

Norwegian Sea

Barents Sea

Karskoye More

Novaya Zemlya

Ostrov Vaygach

Ostrov Kolguyev

Vorkuta

Usa

Arctic Circle

Ural Mountains

RUSSIAN FEDERATION

Pechora

Syktyvkar

Mezen'

Pinega

Arkhangel'sk

Severnaya Dvina

Kotlas

Kol'skiy Poluostrov

Beloye More

Murmansk

Vologda

Yaroslavl'

Onega

Petrozavodsk

Onezhskoye Ozero

Cherepovets

Tver'

NORWAY

SWEDEN

FINLAND

Ladozhskoye Ozero

Rybinskoye Vdkhr.

Smolensk

St Petersburg

Novgorod

Nevel'

Pskov

Baltic Sea

Gulf of Finland

ESTONIA

LATVIA

LITHUANIA

BELARUS

Arctic Circle

0 km   400

0 miles   400

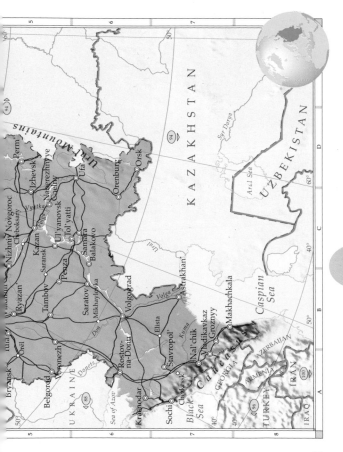

CONTINENTAL NORTH & WEST ASIA

ARCTIC OCEAN

Franz Josef Land

Svalbard
(Norway)

Novaya Zemlya

Kara
Sea

Yamal
Peninsula

Barents
Sea

Arctic Circle

RUSSIAN F

Ural Mts.

Ob'

Yenisey

West Siberian
Plain

Baltic
Sea

North European Plain

Volga

Ural Mountains

EUROPE

Central Russian
Upland

Danube

Volga

Don

KAZAKHSTAN

Kazakh
Uplands

Ob'

Altai Mts.

Bosporus

Black Sea

AZERBAIJAN

GEORGIA

Kirghiz
Steppe

L. Balkhash

Aral
Sea

Syr Darya

Kyzyl Kum

Dardanelles

ARMENIA

Caspian
Sea

UZBEKISTAN

Amu Darya

Ten Shan
Pik Pobedy 14,407ft

TURKEY

Mt. Ararat
16,805ft

Kara Kum

TURKMENISTAN

KYRGYZSTAN

Communism Peak 24,591ft

TAJIKISTAN

Euphrates

18,387ft

Tigris

IRAN

Iranian
Plateau

Hindu Kush

AFGHANISTAN

Mediterranean
Sea

CYPRUS

LEBANON

ISRAEL

SYRIA

Syrian
Desert

A S

Dead Sea
-1,322ft

IRAQ

JORDAN

KUWAIT

An Nafud

Suez Canal

Persian Gulf

BAHRAIN

QATAR

Zagros Mts.

Brahmaputra

U.A.E.

Gulf of Oman

Indus

Tropic of Cancer

Nile

Arabian Peninsula

SAUDI
ARABIA

OMAN

AFRICA

Red Sea

Rub' al Khali

Arabian
Sea

Bay
of
Bengal

YEMEN

Gulf of Aden

Socotra
(Yemen)

0 km   1000

0 miles   1000

ARCTIC OCEAN

ernaya Zemlya

New Siberian Islands

Laptev Sea

East Siberian Sea

Wrangel I.

Taymyr Peninsula

Limit of permanent pack-ice

Central Siberian Plateau

Chukchi Sea

eria

Verkhoyansk Range

Chersky Range

Arctic Circle

ERATION

Kolyma Range

Bering Strait

Lena

Lena

ara

Stanovoy Range

Dzhugdzhur Range

Sea of Okhotsk

Kamchatka ▲ 4750m

Bering Sea

Amur

L. Baikal

Sakhalin

Aleutian Islands (USA)

Sikhote-Alin Range

Sea of Japan

Hokkaidō

PACIFIC

ng River

Honshū

Yangtze

Kyushu

OCEAN

Hawaiian Is. (USA)

Tropic of Cancer

Mekong

Hainan Dao

Taiwan

Northern Marianas (USA)

Mariana Trench

South China Sea

Luzon

Guam (USA)

93

RUSSIA & KAZAKHSTAN

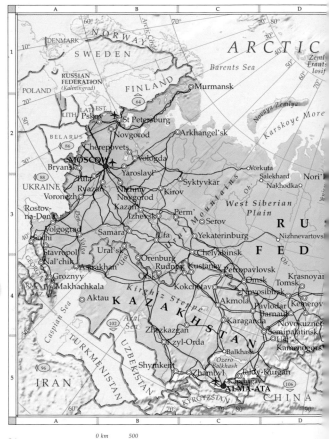

0 km 500

0 miles 500

TURKEY, CYPRUS & THE CAUCASUS

ROMANIA
BULGARIA
GREECE

Danube

Black Sea

Edirne
Kırklareli
Tekirdağ
Bosporus
Kâğıthane
İstanbul
İzmit
Zonguldak
Küre Dağları
Kastamonu
Sinop
Samsu
Marmara Denizi
Karabük
Adapazarı
Çankırı
Kızıl Irmak
Çorum
Çalık Dağları
Or
Dardanelles
Bursa
Çanakkale
40°
Eskişehir
ANKARA
Tokat
Si
Balıkesir
Kütahya
Yozgat
Ayvalık
Lesbos (Greece)
Manisa
Uşak
Afyon
TURK
Chios
İzmir
Nevşehir
Kayseri
R
Samos
Aydın
Denizli
Isparta
Tuz Gölü
Konya
Niğde
Kahram maraş
Muğla
Bodrum
Antalya
Ereğli
Osmaniye
Adana
Gazian
Toros Dağları
Tarsus
Mersin
İskenderun
Dalaman
Antalya Körfezi
Antakya
Rhodes (Greece)
Kárpathos (Greece)
TURKISH REPUBLIC OF NORTHERN CYPRUS
Girne (Kyrenia)
Gazimağusa (Famagusta)
NICOSIA
Larnaca
Paphos
Limassol
Mediterranean Sea
Crete (Greece)
CYPRUS
LEBANON

30°
30°
88
84
84
84

0 km   200

0 miles   200

THE NEAR EAST

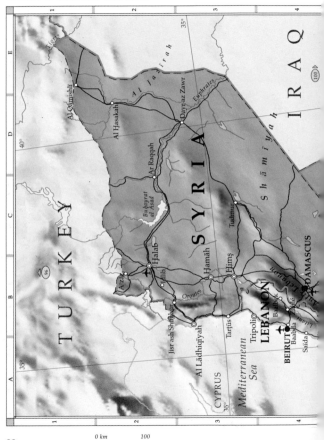

IRAQ

SYRIA

TURKEY

Al Jazīrah

Tigris

Euphrates

Al Qāmishli

Al Ḥasakah

Dayr az Zawr

Ar Raqqah

Buḥayrat al Asad

Shāmiyah

Tudmur

Ḥalab

Idlib

A'zāz

Ḥamāh

Ḥimṣ

Orontes

Jisr ash Shughūr

Al Lādhiqīyah

Ṭarṭūs

Tripoli

LEBANON

BEIRUT

Baalbek

Zaḥle

Ba'abda

Ṣaidā

DAMASCUS

Mediterranean Sea

CYPRUS

98

0 km   100

0 miles   100

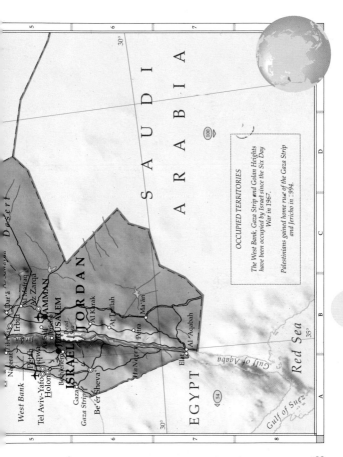

OCCUPIED TERRITORIES

The West Bank, Gaza Strip and Golan Heights have been occupied by Israel since the Six Day War in 1967.

Palestinians gained home rule of the Gaza Strip and Jericho in 1994.

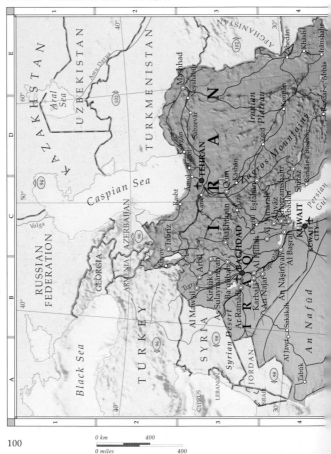

0 km   400

0 miles   400

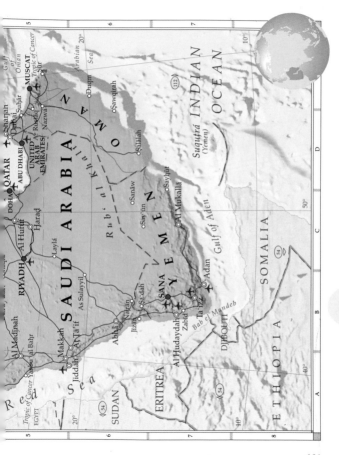

CENTRAL ASIA

KAZAKHSTAN

Aral Sea

Ustyurt Plateau

Sur Darya

UZBEKISTAN

Nukus
Keneurgench
Tel'mansk
Dashkhovuz
Urgench
Turtkul'

Uchkuduk
Zarafshan
Ozero Aydarku

Caspian

Zaliv Kara-Bogaz-Gol

TURKMENISTAN

Karakumy

Turan Lowland

Turkmenbashy
Cheleken
Nebitdag
Gazandzhyk
Gyzylarbat

Bukhara
Seydi
Chardzhev
Komsomol'sk
Sayat

Nav
Samarka
Karshi

Bakherden
Gökdepe
Byuzmeyin
ASHGABAT
Kaka
Karakumskiy Kanal
Tedzhen

Amu Darya
Kerki

Sea

Mary
Bayramaly
Yëloten

Murgab

Aqchah
Shebenghan
Mazar-e Sha
Meymaneh
Bala Morghab
Gushgy
Qal'eh-ye Now

Bandee Torkestan

Morghab

I R A N

Herat

Harirud

AFGHANISTAl

Farah

Gereshk
Kandahar
Kal

Zaranj
Dasht-e Margow
Helmand

50°
60°

40°

30°

60°

0 km   200

0 miles   200

Aksai Chin
Occupied by China,
claimed by India.

Jammu & Kashmir
A "line of control" was agreed
between India and Pakistan in
1972.

Demchok/Dêmqog
Claimed by India
and China.

EAST & SOUTH ASIA

ASIA

Aral Sea

Caspian Sea

Lake Baikal

14,312ft

Altai Mountains

MONGOLIA

Gobi

Tien Shan

14,407ft

Turpan Depression
-505ft

Takla Makan

Hindu Kush

Altun Mts.

CHINA

Kunlun Mts.

Yellow Riv.

Great Plain
of China

Iranian
Plateau

24,757ft

Himalayas

Plateau of Tibet

PAKISTAN

NEPAL

BHUTAN

Indus

Thar
Desert

Mt. Everest
29,030ft

Ganges Plain

Ganges

BANGLADESH

Yangtze

Hong Kong

Macao
(Portugal)

Tropic of Cancer

Indus
Delta

INDIA

Ganges
Delta

MYANMAR

Hainan
Dao

Arabian
Peninsula

Arabian
Sea

Godavari

Deccan

Western Ghats

Bay
of
Bengal

Irrawaddy

Mekong

THAILAND

VIETNAM

LAOS

South
China
Sea

Lakshadweep
(India)

Eastern Ghats

Andaman Is.
(India)

Andaman
Sea

Gulf
of
Thailand

CAMBODIA

13,455ft

MALDIVES

SRI
LANKA

Nicobar Is.
(India)

MALAYSIA

BRUNEI

Equator

SINGAPORE

Borneo

Str. of Malacca

Sumatra

12,467ft

Java Sea

IND

INDIAN
OCEAN

Krakatau
2,667ft

Java

Bali

Java Trench

0 km   1000

0 miles   1000

Amur

Sea
of
Okhotsk

Sakhalin

Aleutian Islands (USA)

Manchurian
Plain

Kurile Tr.

Kurile Trench

Emperor Seamounts

NORTH
KOREA

Sea
of
Japan

Hokkaidō

SOUTH
KOREA

JAPAN

Honshū

Yellow
Sea

Korea Strait

▲Mt. Fuji
12,399ft

Hawaiian Islands (USA)

East
China
Sea

Kyūshū

Ryukyu Islands
(Japan)

Tropic of Cancer

AIWAN

Luzon Strait

Northern Marianas Is.
(USA)

122

PACIFIC

Guam (USA)

Marshall
Islands

OCEAN

HILIPPINES

Mariana Trench

Micronesia

Caroline
Islands

Melanesia

Equator

elebes
ea

Moluccas

Bismarck
Archipelago

Celebes

E S I A

16,503ft

New Guinea

Banda Sea

res

Arafura
Sea

Timor

Solomon
Islands

124

Timor
Sea

AUSTRALASIA

WESTERN CHINA & MONGOLIA

RUSSIAN FED

KAZAKHSTAN

Lake
Balkhash

KYRGYZSTAN

TAJIKISTAN

Kashi

PAKISTAN

Aksai Chin
Occupied by
China, claimed
by India.

Demchok/Dêmqog
Claimed by
India and China

INDIA

Altay

Irtysh

Karamay

Dzungaria

Yining

Kuytun

ÚRÚMQI

Tien Shan

Korla

Tarim He

XINJIANG

Tarim Pendi

Taklimakan
Shamo

Hotan

Altun Shan

Kunlun Shan

Qing-Zang
Gaoyuan

Gar

Tangra Yumco

Siling
Co

Brahmaputra

Xigaze

Himalayas

NEPAL

Uvs
Nuur

Ulaangom

Hyargas
Nuur

Hovd

Altay

Altai Mountains

Hami

Lop Nur

Qilian Shan

Golmud

CHI

Tongtian He

Tanggula Shan

Naqqu

Salween

LHASA

TIBET

BHUTAN

INDIA

Hôvsgôl
Nuur

Selenge Gol

Tsetserleg

MON

G

Qinghai
Hu

Yushu

Qamdo

MYANMAR

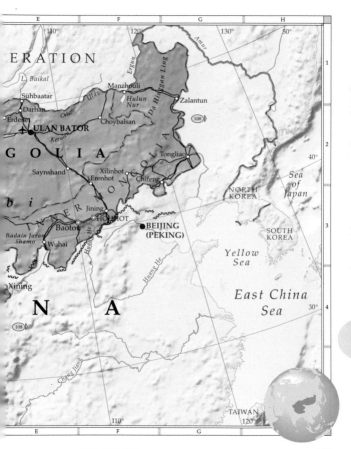

ERATION

L. Baikal

Sühbaatar

Darhan

Erdenet

ULAN BATOR

Orhon

Kerulen

G O L I A

Saynshand

b i

Manzhouli

Hulun Nur

Choybalsan

Xilinhot

Erenhot

Zalantun

108

Tongliao

Chifeng

NORTH KOREA

Sea of Japan

40°

SOUTH KOREA

I N N E R M O N G O L I A

Jining

HOHHOT

Baotou

Badain Jaran Shamo

Wuhai

BEIJING (PEKING)

Huang He

Yellow Sea

Xining

N **A**

Huang He

East China Sea

30°

108

Chang Jiang

TAIWAN

E 110°

F 120°

G 130°

H 50°

1

2

3

4

E 110°

F 110°

G 120°

EASTERN CHINA & KOREA

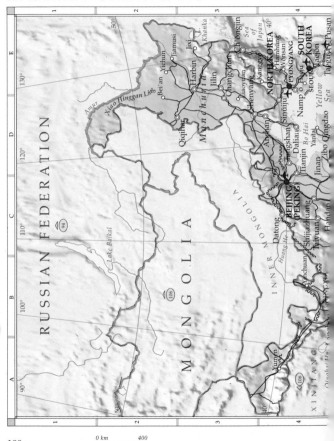

0 km   400

0 miles   400

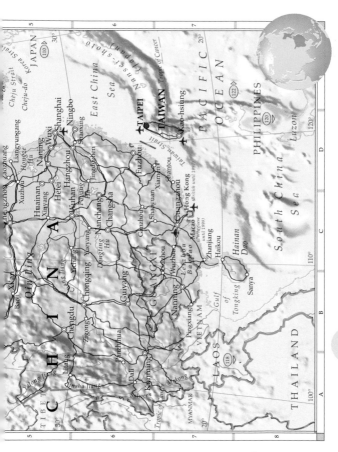

JAPAN

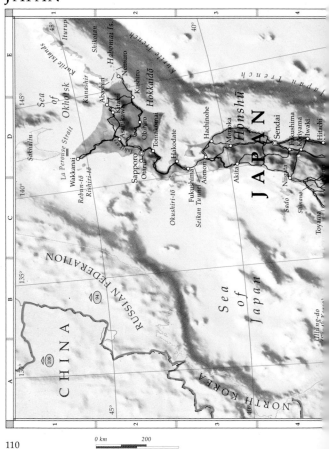

0 km 200

0 miles 200

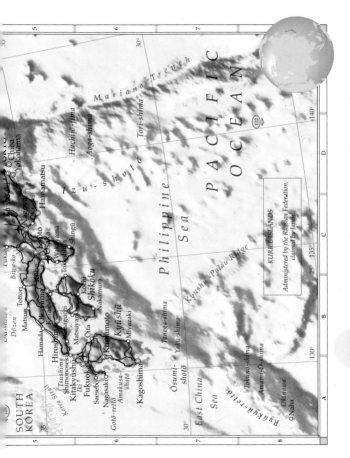

SOUTH
KOREA

Ōki-shotō
Dōzen
Tottori
Hamada
Matsue
Yonago
Tsushima
Iki
Kitakyūshū
Shimonoseki
Fukuoka
Saseho
Nagasaki
Goto-rettō
Amakusa-
shotō
Kagoshima
Ōsumi-
shotō

Bitau-ko
Okayama
Hiroshima
Yamaguchi
Ōita
Matsuyama
Kumamoto
Miyazaki
Yaku-shima

Fukui
Kyōto
Ōsaka
Wakayama
Kōchi
Tokushima
Nakamura
Shikoku
Kyūshū

Nagoya
Toyohashi
Shingū

Hamamatsu

Izu-shotō

Hachijō-jima

Aoga-shima

Tori-shima

Chiba
Yokohama

Mariana Trench

Fune ga-shima

Tanega-shima

Tokuno-shima
Amami-O-shima

Ryūkyū-rettō

Okinawa
Naha

East China
Sea

PACIFIC
OCEAN

Philippine
Sea

Kyushu-Palau Ridge

KURILE ISLANDS
Administered by the Russian Federation,
claimed by Japan.

122

30°

140°

135°

130°

25

30°

35°

111

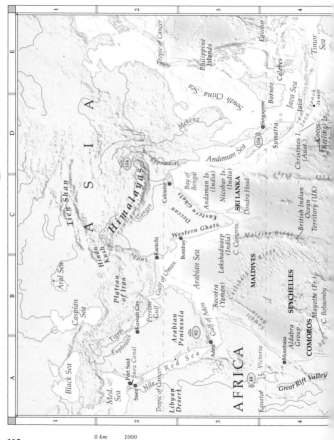

Tropic of Cancer

Equator

Philippine Islands

Borneo

Celebes

Timor Sea

Java Sea

South China Sea

Java

Mekong

Trench 24,450

A S I A

Tien Shan

Andaman Sea

Sumatra

Singapore

Christmas I. (Austr.)

Cocos (Keeling) Is.

East 104

Appalachian

H I M A L A Y A S

104

Bay of Bengal

Andaman Is. (India)

Nicobar Is. (India)

SRI LANKA

Dondra Head

Hindu Kush

Ganges

Calcutta

Deccan

Eastern Ghats

British Indian Ocean Territory (UK)

East Indian Ridge

Aral Sea

Plateau of Iran

Karachi

Indus

Western Ghats

Bombay

C. Comorin

Maldive Ridge

Mid Indian Ridge

Caspian Sea

Lakshadweep (India)

MALDIVES

SEYCHELLES

Black Sea

Tigris

Euphrates

Gulf of Oman

Persian Gulf

Kuwait City

Arabian Sea

Socotra (Yemen)

Mayotte (Fr.)

C. Bobaomby

COMOROS

Arabian Peninsula

92

Gulf of Aden

Aden

Mombasa

Aldabra Group

Mid Indian Ridge

Port Said

Suez Canal

Suez

Nile

Red Sea

AFRICA

Victoria

48

Great Rift Valley

Med. Sea

Tropic of Cancer

Libyan Desert

Equator

0 km   1000

0 miles   1000

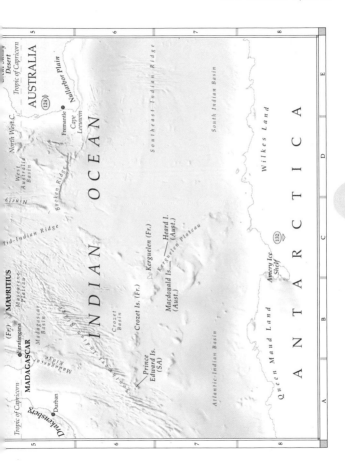

AUSTRALIA
(124)

Great Sandy Desert
Tropic of Capricorn
North West C.
West Australia Basin
Ninety
Broken Ridge
Mid-Indian Ridge
Fremantle
Cape Leeuwin
Nullarbor Plain

Southeast Indian Ridge

South Indian Basin

WILKES LAND

ANTARCTICA

INDIAN OCEAN

MAURITIUS
(Fr.)
Mascarene Plateau
Farafangana
MADAGASCAR
Madagascar Basin
Southwest Indian Ridge
Prince Edward Is. (SA)
Crozet Basin
Crozet Is. (Fr.)
Kerguelen (Fr.)
Heard I. (Aust.)
Kerguelen Plateau
Macdonald Is. (Aust.)
Atlantic-Indian Basin
Amery Ice Shelf
(132)
Queen Maud Land

Tropic of Capricorn
Durban
Drakensberg

113

NORTH INDIA, PAKISTAN & BANGLADESH

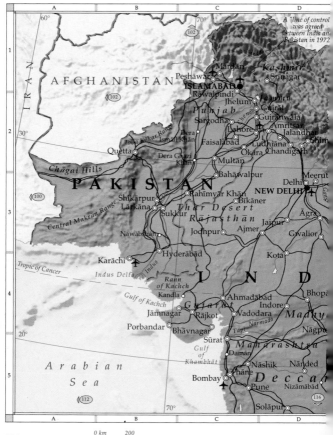

A line of control was agreed between India and Pakistan in 1972

IRAN

AFGHANISTAN

Peshāwar · Mardān · Kashmir · Srīnagar

ISLAMABAD

Rāwalpindi · Jhelum · Jammu

Punjab

Sargodha · Gujrāt · Gujrānwāla

Chenab

Dera Ismāīl Khān · Lahore · Amritsar · Jalandhar

Tobā Kākar Range

Faisalābād · Ludhiāna · Chandīgarh · Shiml

Quetta · Okāra

Dera Ghāzi Khān · Multān · Meerut

Chāgai Hills

Bahāwalpur · Delhi

PAKISTAN

NEW DELHI

Shikārpur · Rahīmyār Khān · Bīkāner

Larkāna · Thar Desert

Central Makrān Range · Sukkur · Rājasthān · Jaipur · Āgra

Nawābshāh · Jodhpur · Ajmer · Gwalior

Kota

Karāchi · Hyderābad · I · N · D

Tropic of Cancer · Indus Delta · Indus

Raun of Kachch

Gulf of Kachch · Kandla · Ahmadābād · Bhopā

Gujarāt · Indore · Madhy

Jāmnagar · Rājkot · Vadodara

Porbandar · Bhāvnagar · Nāgpu

Narmada

Sūrat · Tāpi · Mahārāshtra

Gulf of Khambhāt · Daman

Arabian Sea · Nāshik · Nānded · Deccar

Bombay · Thāne

Pune · Nizāmābād

Solāpur

0 km 200

0 miles 200

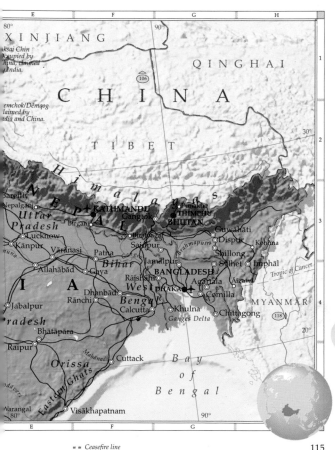

80°

XINJIANG

ksai Chin
ccupied by
hina, claimed
India.

QINGHAI

106

C H I N A

emchok/Dêmqog
laimed by
dia and China.

90°

T I B E T

30°

H i m a l a y a s

N E P A L

Bareilly
Nepalganj
KATHMANDU
Birganj
Gangtok
Punakha
THIMPHU
BHUTAN

Uttar
Pradesh
Lucknow
Biratnagar
Guwāhāti
Dispur
Kohīma
Kānpur
Varanasi
Patna
Saidpur
Jamalpur
Brahmaputra
Shillong
Imphāl
Allahābād
Ganges
Bihar
Gaya
BANGLADESH
Sylhet
Rājshāhi
West
DHAKA
Agartala
Āīzawl
Tropic of Cancer
Jabalpur
Dhanbād
Ranchi
Bengal
Comilla
MYANMAR
Pradesh
Bhātāpāra
Khulna
Calcutta
Chittagong
118
20°
Raipur
Ganges Delta
Orissa
Mahanadi
Cuttack
B a y
o f
B e n g a l
Eastern Ghats
Warangal
80°
Visākhapatnam
90°

= = Ceasefire line

115

SOUTHERN INDIA

Arabian Sea

Arabian Basin

Bombay
Thane   Nānded
Pune   Nizāmābād
114
Deccan
Solāpur
Hyderābād
INDIA
Belgaum   *Karnātaka*
Pānāji   Hubli
Goa
Dāvangere   Kurnool   *Andhra Pradesh*
Bangalore   Vellore
Mangalore   Mysore   *Tami*
Salem   *Nādu*

Amīndīvi Is.
Lakshadweep
(India)

Kavaratti I.
Calicut
Coimbatore
Tiruchch-
Ernākulam   *Kerala*   rāppal

Kalpeni I.
Cochin
Madura
Dhanushkoc

Minicoy I.
Trivandrum   *Gulf of Manna*
Nāgercoil

112

Thiladhunmathi Atoll

MALDIVES

MALE'

Kolhumadulu Atoll

Maldive Ridge

Equator

Huvadhu Atoll

IND

0 km   300

0 miles   300

80°
90°
118
MYANMAR
Varangal
Visākhapatnam
Eastern Ghats
Irrawaddy Delta
Rajahmundry
Vijayawāda
B a y
Andaman Is.
(India)
Ongole
o f
North Andaman
Nellore
B e n g a l
Middle Andaman
Madras
Port Blair
Andaman-Nicobar Ridge
Māmallapuram
South Andaman
Andaman
Sea
Pondicherry
Little Andaman
10°
alk Strait
affna
SRI LANKA
Trincomalee
nnar
Nicobar Is.
Batticaloa
(India)
Kandy
Great Nicobar
COLOMBO
alle
Matara
120
Sumatra
C e y l o n   P l a i n
Ninetyeast Ridge
0°
N   O C E A N
Equator
112
90°

117

MAINLAND SOUTHEAST ASIA

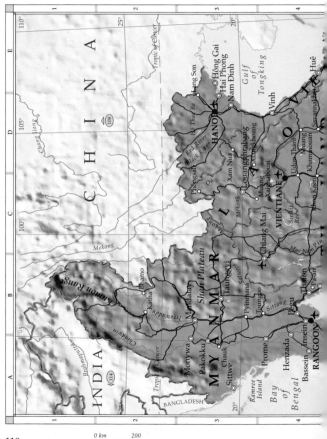

0 km 200

0 miles 200

MARITIME SOUTHEAST ASIA

MYANMAR

Gulf of Tongking

Hainan Dao

THAILAND

LAOS

VIETNAM

Andaman Sea

CAMBODIA

South China Sea

Gulf of Thailand

Spratly Is. (Disputed)

Nicobar Is. (India)

Banda Aceh

Balabac S

George Town

Kota Bharu

Kota Kinabalu

BANDAR SERI BEGAWAN

P. Pinang

Kuala Terengganu

Taiping

BRUNEI

Medan

Ipoh

Kep. Natuna (Indonesia)

Pematangsiantar

Kelang

Kuantan

Danau Toba

Seremban

KUALA LUMPUR

MALAYSIA

Tah

Kuching

Sarawak

Melaka

Borneo

Sumatra

Johor Bharu

SINGAPORE

Peg. Muller

Equator

Kep. Banyak

Pakambaru

Pontianak

Kapuas

Samarinda

Padang

Kep. Lingga

Balikpapan

Jambi

P. Bangka

Kep. Mentawai

Pangkalpinang

Banjarmasin

Bengkulu

P. Belitung

Palembang

Java Sea

Tanjungkarang

I N D

JAKARTA

Java

Bogor

Cirebon

Semarang

Surabaya

Bandung

Malang

Bali

Yogyakarta

Jember

Denpa

INDIAN OCEAN

Java Trench

0 km   400

0 miles   400

THE PACIFIC OCEAN

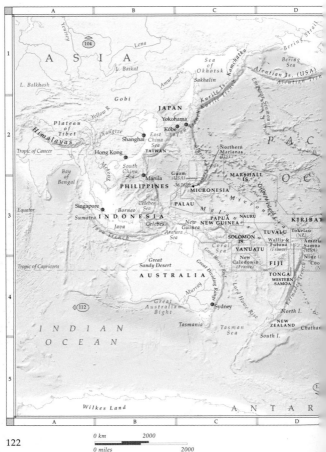

ASIA

Yenisey

Lena

L. Baikal

L. Balkhash

Amur

Sea of Okhotsk

Sakhalin

Kamchatka

Bering Strait

Bering Sea

Aleutian Is. (USA)

Aleutian Trench

Gobi

Yellow R.

Plateau of Tibet

Himalayas

Yangtze

Mekong

Tropic of Cancer

Hong Kong

Shanghai

East China Sea

JAPAN

Yokohama

Kōbe

Kuril Is.

Kuril Trench

Northern Marianas (USA)

PAC

O C

Emperor Seamount

Bay of Bengal

South China Sea

TAIWAN

Manila

Guam (USA)

−36,163ft

MARSHALL IS.

Equator

Singapore

Sumatra

Borneo

Celebes Sea

PHILIPPINES

PALAU

MICRONESIA

Micro

Java

INDONESIA

Celebes

New Guinea

PAPUA NEW GUINEA

NAURU

KIRIBAT

Java Trench

Arafura Sea

Mel

Coral Sea

SOLOMON IS.

VANUATU

TUVALU

Wallis & Futuna (France)

Tokelau (NZ)

Amer Samo (US)

Tropic of Capricorn

Great Sandy Desert

New Caledonia (France)

FIJI

Niue Coo (N

AUSTRALIA

Great Dividing Range

Lord Howe Rise

TONGA

WESTERN SAMOA

Murray

Sydney

North I.

Kermadec Trench

Great Australian Bight

Tasmania

Tasman Sea

NEW ZEALAND

Chatha

INDIAN

OCEAN

South I.

Wilkes Land

ANTAR

0 km   2000

0 miles   2000

AUSTRALASIA & OCEANIA

0 km   1000

0 miles   1000

MARSHALL IS.

Kingman Reef *(USA)*

Palmyra Atoll *(USA)*

Baker & Howland Is. *(USA)*

Jarvis Island *(USA)*

Equator

104

P A C I F I C   O C E A N

ronesia

AURU

Gilbert Is.

K I R I B A T I

Phoenix Is.

Line Islands

P o l y n e s i a

TUVALU

Tokelau *(New Zealand)*

Northern Cook Is.

Marquesas Is.

WESTERN SAMOA

Wallis & Futuna *(France)*

American Samoa *(USA)*

Cook Islands *(New Zealand)*

French Polynesia *(France)*

NUATU

Vanua Levu

Niue *(New Zealand)*

Tahiti

Viti Levu

iles Loyauté

TONGA

FIJI

Southern Cook Is.

Society Islands

Tropic of Capricorn

South Fiji Basin

Norfolk I. *(Australia)*

Kermadec Islands *(NZ)*

122

North Cape

Bay of Plenty

East Cape

P A C I F I C   O C E A N

North I.

Kermadec Trench

NEW ZEALAND

Cook Strait

South I.

Chatham I. *(NZ)*

Cook ▲ 350ft

Canterbury Bight

aveaux Strait

art I.

Southwest Pacific Basin

uckland I. *(NZ)*

125

THE SOUTHWEST PACIFIC

MARSHALL ISLANDS

Guam (USA)   Agana

Ralik Chain   Ratak Chain

Micronesia   Majuro

Mariinas Trench

Yap   Caroline Islands

Chuuk Is.   Pohnpei I.

KOROR   PALIKIR

PALAU   Kosrae

MICRONESIA   NAURU

0° Equator

PAPUA NEW GUINEA

Bismarck Archipelago   New Ireland

INDONESIA   New Guinea   Madang   Bougainville I.   New Georgia

Mendi   Lae   New Britain

PORT MORESBY   Solomon Sea   HONIARA   Santa Cruz Is.

Arafura Sea   Torres Strait   SOLOMON ISLANDS

Melanesia

Arnhem Land   Gulf of Carpentaria   Coral Sea   VANUATU

Bank

NORTHERN TERRITORY   Cooktown   Coral Sea Islands (Australia)   PORT-V

Tennant Creek   Cairns   New Caledonia (France)

Mount Isa   Normanton   Townsville   Noumea   Îles Loya

AUSTRALIA   Cloncurry   Mackay   Great Dividing Range

Alice Springs   Longreach   QUEENSLAND   Rockhampton

Great Barrier Reef   Bundaberg

0 km   400

0 miles   400

PACIFIC OCEAN

International Date Line

Kingman Reef (USA)

Palmyra Atoll (USA)

Baker & Howland Is. (USA)

Teraina
Tabuaeran

Jarvis I. (USA)

Kiritimati

Equator

Line Islands

BAIRIKI
Tarawa
naba

Gilbert Islands

KIRIBATI

Phoenix Islands

TUVALU

FONGAFALE

Tokelau
(New Zealand)

Vostok I.

Caroline I.

WESTERN SAMOA

American Samoa (USA)

Flint I.

Northern Cook Is.

Wallis & Futuna (France)

APIA

Pago Pago

French Polynesia (France)

Polynesia

FIJI

Vanua Levu

Vava'u Group

Niue (NZ)

Cook Islands (New Zealand)

Îles de la Société

Viti Levu

SUVA

Ha'apai Group

Alofi

Southern Cook Is.

Papeete

Tahiti

NUKU'ALOFA

Avarua

TONGA

Rarotonga

International Date Line

Tropic of Capricorn

127

WESTERN AUSTRALIA

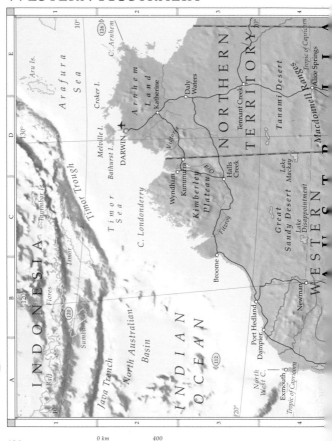

0 km   400

0 miles   400

SOUTHEAST AUSTRALIA

0 km   400

0 miles   400

NEW ZEALAND

North Cape

PACIFIC

OCEAN

Kaitaia

Whangarei

T a s m a n

S e a

Auckland

Coromandel

Hamilton

Bay of Plenty

Tauranga

East Cape

North Island

Rotorua

Taupo

Raukumara Range

New Plymouth

L. Taupo

Gisborne

NEW

Napier

ZEALAND

Wanganui

Hastings

Cook Strait

Palmerston North

Masterton

Nelson

WELLINGTON

Westport

Blenheim

Greymouth

Kaikoura

Campbell Plateau

South Island

Southern Alps

Christchurch

Canterbury Plains

Ashburton

Canterbury Bight

Milford Sound

Timaru

Queenstown

Hampden

Lumsden

PACIFIC

Invercargill

Dunedin

Foveaux Strait

OCEAN

Stewart I.

0 km   200

0 miles   200

ANTARCTICA

ATLANTIC OCEAN

ATLANTIC

Scotia Ridge

Brazillian zone of interest

British Antarctic Territory (UK)

Falkland Is. (UK)

South Shetland Is. (UK)

South Orkney Is. (UK)

Cape Horn

Drake Passage

Antarctic Peninsula

Bellingshausen Sea

Chilean Claim

Argentina Claim

Weddell Sea

Ronne Ice Shelf

Alexander I.

Graham Land

Vinson Massif ▲ 16,864ft

Ellsworth Land

Antarctic Circle

Amundsen Sea

Pine Island Bay

Marie Byrd Land

Lesser Antarctica

Mt. Sidley ▲ 13,718ft

Peter the First I. (Norway)

Average extent of winter sea ice

PACIFIC OCEAN

Southeast Pacific Basin

Queen

Ritser-Larsen Ice Shelf

ANTA

Berkner I.

South Pola Plateau

Transantarctic Mountains

Sout Pole

Mount Kirkpatrick ▲ 14,856ft
Mt. Markham 14,276f

Ross Ice Shelf

Cape Colbeck

Limit of permanent pack ic

Ross Sea

Ross Dependency

0 km   750

0 miles   750

E   F   G   H

OCEAN

Limit of permanent pack ice

Maud Land (Norway)

Lutzow-Holm Bay

Enderby Land

Average extent of winter sea ice

R C T I C A

A u s t r a l i a n   A n t a r c t i c

Cape Darnley

Mackenzie Bay

Lambert Glacier

Prydz Bay

Princess Elizabeth Land

Kerguelen Plateau

Greater
Antarctica

T e r r i t o r y

Antarctic Circle

Shackleton Ice Shelf

Davis Sea

ustralian Antarctic Territory

Cape Poinsett

▲ *Mt. Erebus 12,448ft*

INDIAN

OCEAN

Terre Adélie (France)

Wilkes Land

③④)

*urdo
ound*

▲ *Mt. Siple 11,811ft*

Victoria Land

NZ)

Balleny Is.

*Southwest
Pacific Basin*

E   F   G

GLOSSARY OF ABBREVIATIONS

This glossary provides a comprehensive guide to the abbreviations used in this Atlas.

abbrev. abbreviation
Afgh. Afghanistan
Amh. Amharic
anc. ancient
Ar. Arabic
Arm. Armenia/Armenian
Aus. Austria
Aust. Australia
Az. Azerbaijan/Azerbaijani

Bas. Basque
Bel. Belarus/Belarussian
Belg. Belgium
Bos. & Herz. Bosnia & Herzegovina
Bul. Bulgarian
Bulg. Bulgaria
Bur. Burmese

C Central
C. Cape
Cam. Cambodian
Cast. Castilian
Chin. Chinese
Cord. Cordillera (Spanish for mountain range)
Cz. Czech
Czech Rep. Czech Republic

D.C. District of Columbia
Dan. Danish
Dominican Rep. Dominican Republic

E East
Emb. Embalse
Eng. English
Est. Estonia/Estonian

Faer. Faeroese
Fin. Finnish
Flem. Flemish
Fr. France/French
ft feet

Geo. Georgia
Geor. Georgian
Ger. Germany/German
Gk. Greek

Heb. Hebrew
Hung. Hungary/Hungarian
I. Island
Ind. Indonesian
Is. Islands
It. Italian

Kaz. Kazakh
Kep. Kepulauan (Indonesian/Malay for island group)
Kir. Kirghiz
Kor. Korean
Kurd. Kurdish
Kyrgy. Kyrgyzstan

L. Lake, Lago
Lat. Latin
Latv. Latvian
Leb. Lebanon
Liech. Liechtenstein
Lith. Lithuania/Lithuanian
Lux. Luxembourg

Mac. Macedonia
Med. Sea Mediterranean Sea
Mold. Moldova
Mt. Mount/Mountain
Mts. Mountains

N North
N. Korea North Korea
Neth. Netherlands
NW Northwest
NZ New Zealand

P. Pulau (Indonesian/Malay for island)
Peg. Pegunungan (Indonesian/Malay for mountain range)
Per. Persian
Pol. Poland/Polish
Port. Portuguese
prev. previously

R. River, Rio, Río
Res. Reservoir
Rom. Romania/Romanian
Rus. Russian
Russ. Fed. Russian Federation

S South
S. Korea South Korea
SA South Africa
SCr. Serbo-Croatian
Slvka. Slovakia

Slvna. Slovenia
Som. Somali
Sp. Spanish
St, St. Saint
Str. Strait
Swed. Swedish
Switz. Switzerland

Tajik. Tajikistan
Th. Thai
Turk. Turkish
Turkm. Turkmen
Turkmen. Turkmenistan

U.A.E. United Arab Emirates
UK United Kingdom
Ukr. Ukrainian
USA United States of America
Uzb. Uzbek
Uzbek. Uzbekistan

var. variant
Vdkhr. Vodokhranilishche (Russian for reservoir)
Vdskh. Vodoskhovyshche (Ukrainian for reservoir)
Ven. Venezuela

W West
W. Sahara Western Sahara
Wel. Welsh

Yugo. Yugoslavia

Dorling Kindersley Cartography would like to thank the following for their assistance in producing this Atlas:

James Anderson, Laura Porter, Margaret Hynes, Ruth Duxbury, Roger Bullen, Julie Phillis, Robin Giddings and Tony Chambers.

INDEX

A

135

Albury Australia 130 B3

Alcácer do Sal Portugal 72 C4

Alcalá de Henares Spain 73 E3

Alchevs'k Ukraine 89 G3

Aldabra Group *Island group* Seychelles 59 G1

Aleg Mauritania 52 C3

Aleksandriya *see* Oleksandriya

Aleksandropol' *see* Gyumri

Aleksinac Yugoslavia 80 E4

Alençon France 70 B3

Alessandria Italy 76 A2

Ålesund Norway 65 A5

Aleutian Islands *Islands* Alaska, USA 16 A3

Aleutian Trench *Undersea feature* Pacific Ocean 122 D1

Alexander Island *Island* Antarctica 132 B2

Alexandretta *see* Iskenderun

Alexandria Egypt 54 B1

Alexandria Louisiana, USA 28 B3

Alexandroúpoli Greece 84 D3

Al Fāshir *see* El Fasher

Alföld *Plain* Hungary 79 D7

Algarve *Region* Portugal 72 C4

Algeciras Spain 72 D5 ·

Algeria *Country* N Africa 50-51

Alghero Italy 77 A5

Algiers *Capital of* Algeria 50 D1

Al Ḥasakah Syria 98 D2

Al Ḥillah Iraq *var.* Hilla 100 B3

Al Ḥudaydah Yemen 101 B7

Al Ḥufūf Saudi Arabia 101 C5

Alicante Spain 73 F4

Alice Springs Australia 126 A5 128 E4

Al Jawf Saudi Arabia 100 B4

Al Jazīrah *Region* Iraq/Syria 98 E2

Al Jīzah *see* El Giza

Al Karak Jordan 99 B6

Al Khārijah *see* El Khārga

Al Khums Libya 51 F2

Al Khurṭūm *see* Khartoum

Alkmaar Netherlands 66 C2

Al Kufrah Libya 51 H4

Al Lādhiqīyah Syria *Eng.* Latakia 98 B3

Allahābād India 114 C4

Allenstein *see* Olsztyn

Allentown Pennsylvania, USA 21 F4

Alma-Ata *Capital of* Kazakhstan *Rus./Kaz.* Almaty 95 C5

Al Madīnah Saudi Arabia *Eng.* Medina 100 A5

Al Mafraq Jordan 99 B5

Almalyk Uzbekistan *Uzb.* Olmaliq 103 E2

Al Manāmah *see* Manama

Al Marj Libya 51 G2

Almaty *see* Alma-Ata

Al Mawṣil Iraq *Eng.* Mosul 100 B3

Almelo Netherlands 66 E3

Almería Spain 73 E5

Al Mukallā Yemen 101 C7

Alofi *Capital of* Niue 122 F5

Alor, Kepulauan *Island group* Indonesia 121 E5

Alps *Mountain range* C Europe 60 D4

Al Qāhirah *see* Cairo

Al Qāmishlī Syria *var.* Kamishli 98 E1

Al Qunayṭirah Syria 98 B4

Altai Mountains *Mountain Range* C Asia 106 C2

Altamura Italy 77 E5

Altay China 106 C2

Altay Mongolia 106 D2

Altun Shan *Mountain Range* China 106 B4

Alturas California, USA 24 B4

Al Wajh Saudi Arabia 100 A5

Alytus Lithuania *Pol.* Olita 87 B5

Amakusa-shotō *Island group* Japan 111 A6

Amami-Ō-shima *Island* Japan 111 A8

Amara *see* Al 'Amārah

Amarillo Texas, USA 27 E2

Amazon *River* South America 36 C2

Amazon Delta *Wetland* Brazil 36 D2

Amazonia *Region* C South America 40 C2

Ambanja Madagascar 59 G2

Ambarchik Russian Federation 95 G2

Ambato Ecuador 38 A4

Amboasary Madagascar 59 F4

Ambon Indonesia 121 F4

Ambositra Madagascar 59 G3

Ambriz Angola 58 B1

Ameland *Island* Netherlands 66 D1

American Falls Reservoir *Reservoir* Idaho, USA 24 E4

American Samoa *External territory* USA, Pacific Ocean 122 D3

Amersfoort Netherlands 66 D3

Amiens France 70 C3

Amīndīvi Islands *Island group* India 116 C2

Amirante Islands *Island group* Seychelles 59 H1

Amman *Capital of* Jordan 99 B5

Ammassalik Greenland *var.* Angmagssalik 62 C4

Ammochostos *see* Gazimaǧusa

Āmol Iran 100 C3

Amorgós *Island* Greece 85 D6

Amritsar India 114 D2

Amsterdam *Capital of* Netherlands 66 C3

Amstetten Austria 75 D6

Am Timan Chad 56 C3

Amu Darya *River* C Asia 102 D3

Amundsen Gulf *Sea feature* Canada 17 E2

Amundsen Sea Antarctica 132 B4

Amur *River* E Asia 93 F3 105 E1

Anadolu Dağları *see* Doğu Karadeniz Dağları

Anadyr' Russian Federation 95 H1

Anápolis Brazil 41 F4

Anatolia *Region* SE Europe 83 G3

Anchorage Alaska, USA 16 C3

Ancona Italy 76 C3

Andalucía *Region* Spain 72 D4

Andaman Islands *Island group* India 117 H2 119 A5

Andaman Sea Indian Ocean 112 D3

Andaman-Nicobar Ridge *Undersea feature* Indian Ocean 117 H3

Andes *Mountain range* South America 37 B6

Andijon *see* Andizhan

Andizhan Uzbekistan *Uzb.*
Andijon 103 F2

Andorra *Country* SW Europe
71 B6

Andorra la Vella *Capital of*
Andorra 71 B6

Ándros *Island* Greece 85 C5

Andros Island *Island* Bahamas
34 C1

Angara *River* C Asia 93 E2

Angara Basin *see* Fram Basin

Ángel de la Guarda, Isla *Island*
Mexico 30 B2

Angel Falls *Waterfall* Venezuela
36 C2

Angeles Philippines 121 E1

Ångermanälven *River* Sweden
64 C4

Angers France 70 B4

Anglesey *Island* Wales, UK
69 C5

Angmagssalik *see* Ammassalik

Angola *Country* C Africa 58

Angola Basin *Undersea feature*
Atlantic Ocean 47 D5

Angora *see* Ankara

Angoulême France 71 B5

Angren Uzbekistan 103 E2

Anguilla *External territory* UK,
West Indies 35

Anjouan *Island* Comoros 59 G2

Ankara *Capital of* Turkey *prev.*
Angora 96 C3

Annaba Algeria 51 E1

An Nafūd *Desert region* Saudi
Arabia 100 B4

An Najaf Iraq *var.* Najaf 100 B4

Annapolis Maryland, USA
21 F4

Ann Arbor Michigan, USA
20 C3

An Nāṣiriyah Iraq *var.* Nasiriya
100 C4

Annecy France 71 D5

Anshan China 108 D4

Antakya Turkey *var.* Hatay
96 D4

Antalaha Madagascar 59 G2

Antalya Turkey *prev.* Adalia
96 B4

Antalya, Gulf of *see* Antalya
Körfezi

Antalya Körfezi *Sea feature*
Mediterranean Sea *Eng.* Gulf
of Antalya, *var.* Gulf of Adalia
96 B4

Antananarivo *Capital of*
Madagascar *prev.* Tananarive
59 G3

Antarctica 132-133

Antarctic Peninsula *Peninsula*
Antarctica 132 A2

Antequera Spain 72 D5

Anticosti, Île d' *Island* Canada
19 E3

Antigua *Island* Antigua &
Barbuda 34 D2

Antigua & Barbuda *Country*
West Indies 35

Anti-Lebanon *Mountains*
Lebanon/Syria 98 B4

Antofagasta Chile 44 B2

Antsirañana Madagascar 59 G2

Antsohihy Madagascar 59 G2

Antwerp *see* Antwerpen

Antwerpen Belgium *Eng.*
Antwerp 67 C5

Aoga-shima *Island* Japan 111 D6

Aomori Japan 110 D3

Aorangi *see* Cook, Mount

Aosta Italy 76 A2

Apeldoorn Netherlands 66 D3

Apennines *see* Appennino

Apia *Capital of* Western Samoa
127 F4

Appalachian Mountains
Mountain range E USA 15 F4

Appennino *Mountain range* Italy
Eng. Apennines 60 D5 76 C4

Apure *River* Venezuela 36 B2

Aputiteeq Greenland 62 D3

Aqaba *see* Al 'Aqabah

Aqaba, Gulf of *Sea feature* Red
Sea *Ar.* Khalīj al 'Aqabah
99 A8

'Aqabah, Khalīj al *see* Red Sea

Āqchah Afghanistan
var. Āqcheh 102 D3

Āqcheh *see* Āqchah

Arabian Basin *Undersea feature*
Indian Ocean 116 B2

Arabian Peninsula *Peninsula*
Asia 83 H5 92 B5

Arabian Sea *Indian Ocean*
112 B3

Aracaju Brazil 41 H3

Arad Romania 88 A4

Arafura Sea Asia/Australasia
122 B3

Araguaia *River* Brazil 41 E3

Arāk Iran 100 C3

Araks *see* Aras

Arak's *see* Aras

Aral Sea *Inland sea*
Kazakhstan/Uzbekistan 92 C3

Ararat, Mount *Peak* Turkey *var.*
Great Ararat, *Turk.* Büyükağrı
Dağı 92 B4

Aras *River* SW Asia *Arm.*
Arak's, *Per.* Rūd-e Aras, *Rus.*
Araks, *Turk.* Aras Nehri 97 G3

Aras Nehri *see* Aras

Arauca Colombia 38 C2

Arauca *River*
Colombia/Venezuela 38 C2

Arbatax Italy 77 A5

Arbīl Iraq *Kurd.* Hawlêr 100 B3

Arctic Ocean 16-17

Arda *River* Bulgaria/Greece
84 C3

Ardennes *Region* W Europe
67 D7

Arendal Norway 65 A6

Arensburg *see* Kuressaare

Arequipa Peru 40 B4

Arezzo Italy 76 C3

Argentina *Country* S South
America 44-45

Argentine Basin *Undersea feature*
Atlantic Ocean 47 B6

Argentine claim in Antarctica
132 C2

Argentino, Lago *Lake* Argentina
45 B7

Århus Denmark 65 A7

Arica Chile 44 B1

Arizona *State* USA 26 B2

Arkansas *State* USA 28 B1

Arkansas *River* C USA 15 E4

Arkhangel'sk Russian
Federation 90 C3 94 C2

Arles France 71 D6

Arlon Belgium 67 D8

Armenia *Country* SW Asia 97 G2

Armenia Colombia 38 B3

Armidale Australia 130 E2

Arnhem Netherlands 66 D4

Arnhem, Cape *Coastal feature*
Australia 128 E2

Bābol Iran 100 D3

Babruysk Belarus *Rus.* Bobruysk 87 D6

Bacan, Pulau *Island* Indonesia 121 F4

Bačka Topola Yugoslavia 80 D2

Bacolod Philippines 121 E2

Bacău Romania 88 C4

Badain Jaran Shamo *Desert region* China 107 E3

Badajoz Spain 72 C4

Badalona Spain 73 G2

Baden Switzerland 75 E6

Bādiyat ash Shām *see* Syrian Desert

Bafatá Guinea-Bissau 52 C4

Baffin Bay *Sea feature* Atlantic Ocean 46 B3

Baffin Island *Island* Canada 15 F1

Bafoussam Cameroon 56 B4

Bagdad *see* Baghdad

Bagé Brazil 42 C4

Baghdad *Capital of* Iraq *var.* Bagdad, *Ar.* Baghdād 100 B3

Baghdad *see* Baghdad

Baghlān Afghanistan 103 E4

Baguio Philippines 121 E1

Bahamas *Country* West Indies, Atlantic Ocean 34

Baharden *see* Bakherden

Bahāwalpur Pakistan 114 C3

Bäherden *see* Bakherden

Bahía, Islas de la *Islands* Honduras 32 D2

Bahir Dar Ethiopia 54 C4

Bahrain *Country* SW Asia 101 C5

Baia Mare Romania 88 B3

Bai'an China 108 D2

Baikal, Lake *see* Baykal, Ozero

Bairiki *Capital of* Kiribati 127 E2

Baja Hungary 79 C7

Baja California *Peninsula* Mexico *Eng.* Lower California 30 B2

Bajo Nuevo *Island* Colombia 33 F2

Baker Oregon, USA 24 C3

Baker & Howland Islands *External territory* USA, Pacific Ocean 127 F2

Bakersfield California, USA 25 C7

Bakharden *see* Bakherden

Bakherden Turkmenistan *prev.* Bakharden, *var.* Baharden, *Turkm.* Bäherden 102 B3

Bākhtarān Iran *prev.* Kermānshāh 100 C3

Bakı *see* Baku

Baku *Capital of* Azerbaijan *Az.* Bakı, *var.* Baky 96 A3

Baky *see* Baku

Balabac Strait *Sea feature* South China Sea/Sulu Sea 120 D2

Ba'labakk *see* Balbek

Balakovo Russian Federation 91 C6

Bālā Morghāb Afghanistan 102 D4

Balaton *Lake* Hungary *var.* Lake Balaton, *Ger.* Plattensee 79 C7

Balaton, Lake *see* Balaton

Balbina, Represa *Reservoir* Brazil 40 D2

Baleares, Islas *Island group* Spain *Eng.* Balearic Islands 73 H3 82 C3

Balearic Islands *see* Baleares, Islas

Bali *Island* Indonesia 120 D5

Balıkesir Turkey 96 A3

Balikpapan Indonesia 120 D4

Balkan Mountains *Mountain range* Bulgaria *Bul.* Stara Planina 84 C2

Balkhash Kazakhstan 94 C5

Balkhash, Lake *see* Balkhash, Ozero

Balkhash, Ozero *Lake* Kazakhstan *Eng.* Lake Balkhash 92 C3 94 C5

Ballarat Australia 130 B4

Balleny Islands *Island group* Antarctica 133 E5

Balsas *River* Mexico 31 E5

Bălți Moldova 88 D3

Baltic Port *see* Paldiski

Baltic Sea Atlantic Ocean 65 C7

Baltimore Maryland, USA 21 F4

Baltischport *see* Paldiski

Baltiski *see* Paldiski

Baltiysk Kaliningrad, Russian Federation *prev.* Pillau 86 A4

Bamako *Capital of* Mali 52 D4

Bambari Central African Republic 56 C4

Bamenda Cameroon 56 B4

Banaba *Island* Kiribati *prev.* Ocean Island 127 E2

Banda, Laut *see* Banda Sea

Banda Aceh Indonesia 120 A3

Banda Sea *Sea feature* Pacific Ocean *Ind.* Laut Banda 105 E5 121 F4

Bandar-e 'Abbās Iran 100 D4

Bandar-e Büshehr Iran 100 C4

Bandar Seri Begawan *Capital of* Brunei 120 D3

Bandon Oregon, USA 24 A3

Bandundu Zaire 57 C6

Bandung Indonesia 120 C5

Bangalore India 116 D2

Banggai, Kepulauan *Island group* Indonesia 121 E4

Banghāzī Libya *Eng.* Benghazi 51 G2

Bangka, Pulau *Island* Indonesia 120 C4

Bangkok *Capital of* Thailand *Th.* Krung Thep 119 C5

Bangladesh *Country* S Asia 115

Bangor Northern Ireland, UK 69 B5

Bangor Maine, USA 21 G2

Bangui *Capital of* Central African Republic 57 C5

Bani *River* Mali 52 D3

Banī Suwayf *see* Beni Suef

Banja Luka Bosnia & Herzegovina 80 B3

Banjarmasin Indonesia 120 D4

Banjul *Capital of* Gambia 52 B3

Banks Island *Island* Canada 17 E2

Banks Island *Island* Vanuatu, Pacific Ocean 126 D4

Banská Bystrica Slovakia *Ger.* Neusohl, *Hung.* Besztercebánya 79 C6

Bantry Bay *Sea feature* Ireland 69 A6

Banyak, Kepulauan *Island group* Indonesia 120 A3

Banyo Cameroon 56 B4

Baoji China 109 B5

Baotou China 107 E3

Ba'qūbah C Iraq 100 B3

139

Baracaldo Spain 73 E1
Baranavichy Belarus *Rus.* Baranovichi, *Pol.* Baranowicze 87 C6
Baranovichi *see* Baranavichy
Baranowicze *see* Baranavichy
Barbados *Country* West Indies 35 E4
Barbuda *Island* Antigua & Barbuda 35 G3
Barcelona Spain 73 G2
Barcelona Venezuela 39 E1
Bareilly India 115 E3
Barentsburg Svalbard 63 G2
Barents Sea Arctic Ocean 64 E1
Bari Italy 77 E5
Barinas Venezuela 38 D2
Barisan, Pegunungan *Mountains* Indonesia 120 B4
Bar-le-Duc France 70 D3
Barito *River* Indonesia 120 D4
Barlee, Lake *Lake* Australia 124 B3 129 B 5
Barnaul Russian Federation 94 D4
Barnstaple England, UK 69 C7
Barquisimeto Venezuela 38 D1
Barra *Island* Scotland, UK 68 B3
Barranquilla Colombia 38 B1
Barrow *River* Ireland 69 B6
Barstow California, USA 25 C7
Bartang *River* Tajikistan 103 F3
Bartica Guyana 39 G2
Barysaw Belarus *Rus.* Borisov 87 D5
Basarabeasca Moldova 88 D4
Basel Switzerland 75 A7
Basque Provinces *Region* Spain *Sp.* País Vasco 73 E1
Basra *see* Al Başrah
Bassein Myanmar 118 A4
Basse-Terre *Capital of* Guadeloupe 35 G4
Basseterre *Capital of* St Kitts & Nevis 35 G3
Bass Strait *Sea feature* Australia 130 B4
Bastia Corse, France 71 E7
Bastogne Belgium 67 D7
Bata Equatorial Guinea 56 A5
Batangas Philippines 121 E1
Bătdâmbâng Cambodia 119 D5

Bath England, UK 69 D7
Bathurst Australia 130 C3
Bathurst Canada 19 F4
Bathurst Island *Island* Australia 128 D2
Bathurst Island *Island* Canada 17 F2
Batman Turkey *var.* Iluh 97 F2
Batna Algeria 51 E1
Baton Rouge Louisiana, USA 28 B3
Batticaloa Sri Lanka 117 E3
Bat'umi Georgia 97 F2
Bauchi Nigeria 53 G4
Bauru Brazil 42 D2
Bavarian Alps *Mountains* Austria/Germany 75 C7
Bayamo Cuba 34 C2
Bay City Michigan, USA 20 C3
Baydhabo Somalia 55 D6
Baykal, Ozero *Lake* Russian Federation *Eng.* Lake Baikal 93 E3 95 F4
Bayonne France 71 A6
Bayramaly Turkmenistan 102 C3
Bayrūt *see* Beirut
Beaufort Sea Arctic Ocean 17 E2
Beaufort West South Africa 58 C5
Beaumont Texas, USA 27 H4
Beauvais France 70 C3
Béchar Algeria 50 D2
Be'ér Sheva' Israel 99 A6
Beijing *Capital of* China *var.* Peking 108 C4
Beira Mozambique 59 E3
Beirut *Capital of* Lebanon *var.* Beyrouth, Bayrūt 98 B4
Beja Portugal 72 C4
Béjaïa Algeria 51 E1
Bek-Budi *var.* Karshi
Békéscsaba Hungary 79 D7
Belarus *Country* E Europe *var.* Belorussia 87
Belau see Palau
Belcher Islands *Islands* Canada 18 C2
Beledweyne Somalia 55 D5
Belém Brazil 41 F2
Belfast Northern Ireland, UK 69 B5
Belfort France 70 E4

Belgaum India 116 C1
Belgium *Country* W Europe 67
Belgorod Russian Federation 91 A5
Belgrade *Capital of* Yugoslavia *SCr.* Beograd 80 D3
Belitung, Pulau *Island* Indonesia 120 C4
Belize *Country* Central America 32
Belize City Belize 32 C1
Bella Unión Uruguay 42 B4
Belle Île *Island* France 70 A4
Belle Isle, Strait of *Sea feature* Canada 15 G3 19 H3
Bellevue Washington, USA 24 B2
Bellingham Washington, USA 24 B1
Bellingshausen Sea Antarctica 47 A8 132 A3
Bello Colombia 38 B2
Belluno Italy 76 C2
Bellville South Africa 58 C5
Belmopan *Capital of* Belize 32 C1
Belo Horizonte Brazil 41 G5 43 F1
Belorussia *see* Belarus
Belostok *see* Białystok
Beloye More Arctic Ocean *Eng.* White Sea 61 F1 90 C3
Bend Oregon, USA 24 B3
Bendery *see* Tighina
Bendigo Australia 130 B4
Benevento Italy 77 D5
Bengal, Bay of *Sea feature* Indian Ocean 112 C3
Benghazi *see* Banghāzī
Bengkulu Indonesia 120 B4
Benguela Angola 58 B2
Beni Bolivia 40 C4
Benidorm Spain 73 F4
Beni Mellal Morocco 50 C2
Benin *Country* N Africa *prev.* Dahomey 53
Benin, Bight of *Sea feature* W Africa 53 F5
Benin City Nigeria 53 F5
Beni Suef Egypt *var.* Banī Suwayf 54 B1
Benue *River* Cameroon/Nigeria 53 G4
Beograd *see* Belgrade

Berat Albania 81 B3
Berbera Somalia 54 D4
Berbérati Central African Republic 56 C5
Berdyans'k Ukraine 88 G4
Berezina see Byerazino
Bergamo Italy 76 B2
Bergen Norway 65 A5
Bering Sea Pacific Ocean 122 D1
Bering Strait Sea feature Bering Sea/Chukchi Sea 122 D1
Berkner Island Island Antarctica 132 C2
Berlin Capital of Germany 74 D3
Bermejo River Argentina 44 D2
Bermuda External territory UK, Atlantic Ocean 46 B3
Bern Capital of Switzerland Fr. Berne 75 A7
Berne see Bern
Bertoua Cameroon 57 B5
Besançon France 70 D4
Besztercebánya see Banská Bystrica
Bethlehem West Bank 99 B5
Beuthen see Bytom
Beyrouth see Beirut
Béziers France 71 C6
Bezmein see Byuzmeyin
Bhamo Myanmar 118 B2
Bhātāpāra India 114 C4
Bhāvnagar India 114 C4
Bhōpal India 114 D4
Bhutan Country S Asia 115
Biak, Pulau Island Indonesia 121 G4
Białystok Poland Rus. Belostok 78 E3
Biel Switzerland 75 A7
Bielitz-Biala see Bielsko-Biała
Bielsko-Biała Poland Ger. Bielitz-Biala 79 C5
Bighorn Mountains Mountains C USA 22 C2
Big Spring Texas, USA 27 E3
Bihać Bosnia & Herzegovina 80 B3
Bihār State India 115 F3
Bijelo Polje Yugoslavia 80 D4
Bikāner India 114 C3
Bila Tserkva Ukraine 89 E2
Bilbao Spain 73 E1

Billings Montana, USA 22 C2
Biloxi Mississippi, USA 28 C3
Biltine Chad 56 D3
Binghamton New York, USA 21 F3
Bío Bío River Chile 45 B5
Birāk Libya 51 F3
Biratnagar Nepal 115 F3
Birganj Nepal 115 F3
Birmingham England, UK 69 D6
Birmingham Alabama, USA 28 D2
Birni-Nkonni Niger 53 F3
Birsen see Biržai
Biržai Lithuania Ger. Birsen 86 C4
Biscay, Bay of Sea feature Atlantic Ocean 71 A5 73 E1
Biscay Plain Undersea feature Atlantic Ocean 60 B4
Bishkek Capital of Kyrgyzstan prev. Frunze, Pishpek 103 F2
Bishop California, USA 25 C6
Biskra Algeria 51 E2
Bismarck North Dakota, USA 23 E2
Bismarck Archipelago Island group Papua New Guinea 126 B3
Bissau Capital of Guinea-Bissau 52 B4
Bitola Macedonia 81 D6
Bitterroot Range Mountains NW USA 24 D2
Biwa-ko Lake Japan 111 C5
Bizerte Tunisia 51 E1
Bjelovar Croatia 80 B2
Black Drin River Albania/Macedonia 81 D5
Black Forest see Schwarzwald
Black Hills Mountains C USA 22 D3
Blackpool England, UK 69 C5
Black River River China/Vietnam 118 D3
Black Sea Asia/Europe 61 F1 82 B4
Black Volta River Ghana/Ivory Coast 53 E4
Blackwater River Ireland 69 A6
Blagoevgrad Bulgaria 84 B3
Blagoveshchensk Russian Federation 95 G4

Blanca, Bahía Sea feature Argentina 37 C6
Blantyre Malawi 59 E2
Blenheim New Zealand 131 G3
Blida Algeria 50 D1
Bloemfontein South Africa 58 D4
Blois France 70 C4
Bloomington Indiana, USA 20 C4
Bluefields Nicaragua 33 E3
Blue Mountains Mountains W USA 24 C3
Blue Nile River Ethiopia/Sudan 55 C4
Blumenau Brazil 42 D3
Bo Sierra Leone 52 C4
Boa Vista Brazil 40 D1
Bobo-Dioulasso Burkina 53 E4
Bobruysk see Babruysk
Boca de la Serpiente see Serpent's Mouth, The
Bochum Germany 74 A4
Bodø Norway 64 C3
Bodrum Turkey 96 A4
Bogor Indonesia 120 C5
Bogotá Capital of Colombia 38 B3
Bo Hai Sea feature Yellow Sea 108 D4
Bohemian Forest Region Czech Rep 75 D6
Bohol Island Philippines 121 E2
Boise Idaho, USA 24 D3
Bokhara see Bukhara
Bol Chad 56 B3
Bolivia Country C South America 40-41
Bologna Italy 76 C3
Bolton England, UK 69 D5
Bolzano Italy Ger. Bozen 76 C1
Boma Zaire 57 B7
Bombay India var. Mumbai 115 C5 116 C1
Bomu River Central African Republic/Zaire 57 D5
Bonete, Cerro Peak Chile 37 B5
Bongo, Massif des Upland Central African Republic 56 D4
Bongor Chad 56 C3
Bonn Germany 75 A5
Boosaaso Somalia 54 E4

Borås Sweden 65 B7

Bordeaux France 71 B5

Borger Texas, USA 27 E2

Borisov see Barysaw

Borlänge Sweden 65 C6

Borneo *Island* SE Asia 120-121

Bornholm *Island* Denmark 65 C8

Bosanski Šamac Bosnia & Herzegovina 80 C3

Bosna *River* Bosnia & Herzegovina 80 B3

Bosnia & Herzegovina *Country* SE Europe 80-81

Bosporus *Sea feature* Turkey *Turk.* İstanbul Boğazi 96 B2

Bossangoa Central African Republic 56 C4

Boston Massachusetts, USA 21 G3

Botevgrad Bulgaria 84 C2

Bothnia, Gulf of *Sea feature* Baltic Sea 65 C5

Botoşani Romania 88 C3

Botswana *Country* southern Africa 58

Bouaké Ivory Coast 52 D4

Bouar Central African Republic 56 C4

Bougainville Island *Island* Papua New Guinea 126 C3

Bougouni Mali 52 D4

Boulder Colorado, USA 22 C4

Boulogne-sur-Mer France 70 C2

Bourges France 70 C4

Bourgogne *Region* France *Eng.* Burgundy 70 D4

Bourke Australia 130 B2

Bournemouth England, UK 69 D7

Bouvet Island *External territory* Norway, Atlantic Ocean 47 D7

Bowling Green Kentucky, USA 20 C5

Bozeman Montana, USA 22 B2

Bozen see Bolzano

Brač *Island* Croatia 80 B4

Bradford England, UK 69 D5

Braga Portugal 72 C2

Bragança Portugal 72 C2

Brahmaputra *River* S Asia 106 B5 115 G3

Brăila Romania 88 D4

Brainerd Minnesota, USA 23 F2

Brandon Canada 17 G5

Brasília *Capital of* Brazil 41 F4

Braşov Romania 88 C4

Bratislava *Capital of* Slovakia *Ger.* Pressburg, *Hung.* Pozsony 79 C6

Bratsk Russian Federation 95 E4

Braunau am Inn Austria 75 D6

Braunschweig Germany *Eng.* Brunswick 74 C4

Brazil *Country* South America 40-43

Brazil Basin *Undersea feature* Atlantic Ocean 47 C5

Brazilian Highlands *Upland* Brazil 41 G4

Brazos *River* SW USA 27 G3

Brazzaville *Capital of* Congo 57 B6

Brecon Beacons *Hills* Wales, UK 69 E7

Breda Netherlands 66 D4

Bregenz Austria 75 B7

Bremen Germany 74 B3

Bremerhaven Germany 74 B3

Brescia Italy 76 B2

Breslau see Wrocław

Brest Belarus *Pol.* Brześć nad Bugiem, *prev.* Brześć Litewski, *Rus.* Brest-Litovsk 87 B6

Brest France 70 A3

Brest-Litovsk see Brest

Bretagne *Region* France *Eng.* Brittany 70 A3

Breton Sound *Inlet* Louisiana, USA 28 C4

Brezhnev see Naberezhnyye Chelny

Bria Central African Republic 56 D4

Bridgetown *Capital of* Barbados 35 H5

Brig Switzerland 75 D5

Brighton England, UK 69 E7

Brindisi Italy 77 E5

Brisbane Australia 130 D2

Bristol England, UK 69 D7

British Antarctic Territory *Territory* Antarctica 132 B2

British Columbia *Province* Canada 16-17

British Indian Ocean Territory *External territory* UK, Indian Ocean 112 C4

British Isles *Islands* W Europe 68-69

British Virgin Islands *External territory* UK, West Indies 35

Brittany see Bretagne

Brno Czech Republic *Ger.* Brünn 79 B5

Broken Arrow Oklahoma, USA 27 G1

Broken Hill Australia 130 B3

Broken Ridge *Undersea feature* Indian Ocean 113 D5

Bromberg see Bydgoszcz

Brooks Range *Mountains* Alaska, USA 17 F2

Broome Australia 128 C3

Brownfield Texas, USA 27 E3

Brownsville Texas, USA 27 G5

Bruges see Brugge

Brugge Belgium *Fr.* Bruges 67 A5

Brunei *Country* E Asia 120 D3

Brünn see Brno

Brunswick Georgia, USA 29 E3

Brunswick see Braunschweig

Brusa see Bursa

Brussel see Brussels

Brussels *Capital of* Belgium *Fr.* Bruxelles, *Flem.* Brussel 67 C6

Brüx see Most

Bruxelles see Brussels

Bryan Texas, USA 27 G3

Bryansk Russian Federation 91 A5 94 A2

Brześć Litewski see Brest

Brześć nad Bugiem see Brest

Bucaramanga Colombia 38 C2

Buchanan Liberia 52 C5

Bucharest *Capital of* Romania 88 C5

Budapest *Capital of* Hungary 79 C6

Budweis see České Budějovice

Buenaventura Colombia 38 B3

Buenos Aires *Capital of* Argentina 44 D4

Buenos Aires, Lago *Lake* Argentina/Chile 45 B6

Buffalo New York, USA 21 E3

Bug *River* E Europe 78 E3 88 C1

Bujumbura *Capital of* Burundi
prev. Usumbura 55 B7
Bukavu Zaire 57 E6
Bukhara Uzbekistan *var.*
Bokhara, *Uzb.* Bukhoro 102 D2
Bukhoro *see* Bukhara
Bulawayo Zimbabwe 58 D3
Bulgaria *Country* E Europe 84
Bumba Zaire 57 D5
Bunbury Australia 129 B6
Bundaberg Australia 126 C5
130 C1
Bunia Zaire 57 E5
Buraydah Saudi Arabia 101 B5
Burē Ethiopia 54 C4
Burgas Bulgaria 84 E2
Burgos Spain 73 E2
Burgundy *see* Bourgogne
Burkina *Country* W Africa 53
Burlington Iowa, USA 23 G4
Burlington Vermont, USA 21 F2
Burma *see* Myanmar
Burnie Tasmania 130 B4
Burns Oregon, USA 24 C3
Bursa Turkey *prev.* Brusa 96 B3
Burtnieku Ezers *Lake* Latvia
86 C3
Buru *Island* Indonesia 121 F4
Burundi *Country* C Africa 55
Butembo Zaire 57 E5
Butte Montana, USA 22 B2
Butuan Philippines 121 F2
Buurhakaba Somalia 55 D6
Buyo Reservoir *Reservoir* Ivory
Coast 52 D5
Büyükağrı Dağı *see* Ararat,
Mount
Buzău Romania 88 C4
Bydgoszcz Poland *Ger.*
Bromberg 78 C3
Byerazino *River* Belarus *Rus.*
Berezina 87 B6
Bykhaw Belarus *Rus.* Bykhov
87 D6
Bykhov *see* Bykhaw
Bytom Poland *Ger.* Beuthen
79 C5
Byuzmeyin Turkmenistan *prev.*
Bezmein 102 B3
Byzantium *see* İstanbul

C

Caaguazú Paraguay 42 C2
Cabanatuan Philippines 121 E1
Cabimas Venezuela 38 C1
Cabinda *Exclave* Angola 57 B7
58 B1
Cabot Strait *Sea feature* Atlantic
Ocean 19 G4
Čačak Yugoslavia 80 D4
Cáceres Spain 72 D3
Cachoeiro de Itapemirim Brazil
43 F1
Cadiz Philippines 121 E2
Cádiz Spain 72 D5
Caen France 70 B3
Caernarfon Wales, UK 69 C5
Cagayan de Oro Philippines
121 F2
Cagliari Italy 77 A6
Cahors France 71 B5
Cairns Australia 126 B4
Cairo *Capital of* Egypt *Ar.* Al
Qāhirah, *var.* El Qāhira 54 B1
Čakovec Croatia 80 B2
Calabar Nigeria 53 G5
Calabria *Region* Italy 77 D6
Calafate Argentina 45 B7
Calais France 70 C1
Calais Maine, USA 21 H1
Calama Chile 44 B2
Calbayog Philippines 121 F2
Calcutta India 115 F4
Caldas da Rainha Portugal
72 B3
Caldwell Idaho, USA 25 C3
Caleta Olivia Argentina 45 C6
Calgary Canada 17 E5
Cali Colombia 38 B3
Calicut India *var.* Kozhikode
116 D2
California *State* USA 24-25
California, Golfo de *Sea feature*
Pacific Ocean *Eng.* California,
Gulf of 30 B2 123 F2
Callao Peru 40 A4
Caltagirone Italy 77 D7
Caltanissetta Italy 77 C7
Camagüey Cuba 34 C2
Cambodia *Country* SE Asia
Cam. Kampuchea 118-119
Cambridge England, UK 69 E6

Cameroon *Country* W Africa
56-57
Camiri Bolivia 40 D5
Campbell Plateau *Undersea fea-
ture* Pacific Ocean 131 H4
Campeche Mexico 31 H4
Campeche, Bahía de *Sea feature*
Mexico *Eng.* Gulf of
Campeche 31G4
Campina Grande Brazil 41 H3
Campinas Brazil 41 F5 43 E2
Campo Grande Brazil 41 E5
42 C1
Campos Brazil 41 G5 43 F2
Canada *Country* North America
16-17 18-19
Canada Basin *Undersea feature*
Arctic Ocean *var.* Laurentian
Basin 12 B4
Canadian River *River* SW USA
27 E2
Çanakkale Turkey 96 A2
Çanakkale Boğazı *see*
Dardanelles
Canarias, Islas *Islands* Spain
Eng. Canary Islands 46
C4 50 A2
Canary Basin *Undersea feature*
Atlantic Ocean 46 C4
Canary Islands *see* Canarias,
Islas
Canaveral, Cape *Coastal feature*
Florida, USA 29 F4
Canberra *Capital of* Australia
130 C3
Cancún Mexico 31 H3
Caniapiscau *River* Canada 19 E2
Caniapiscau, Réservoir *Reservoir*
Canada 19 E3
Canik Dağları *Mountains* Turkey
96 D2
Çankırı Turkey 96 C2
Cannes France 71 D6
Canoas Brazil 42 D4
Canterbury England, UK 69 E7
Canterbury Bight *Sea feature*
Pacific Ocean 131 C4
Canterbury Plains *Plain* New
Zealand 131 G4
Cân Thơ Vietnam 119 D6
Canton Ohio, USA 20 D4
Canton *see* Guangzhou
Cape Basin *Undersea feature*
Atlantic Ocean 49 C7 58 B5

Cape Coast Ghana 53 E5

Cape Town South Africa 58 C5

Cape Verde *Country* Atlantic Ocean 52 A3

Cape Verde Basin *Undersea feature* Atlantic Ocean 46 C4

Cape York Peninsula *Peninsula* Australia 124 C2

Cap-Haïtien Haiti 34 D3

Capri, Isola di *Island* Italy 77 C5

Caquetá *River* Colombia 38 C4

CAR *see* Central African Republic

Caracas *Capital of* Venezuela 38 D1

Carazinho Brazil 42 C3

Carbondale Illinois, USA 20 B5

Carcassonne France 71 C6

Cardiff Wales, UK 69 C7

Cardigan Bay *Sea feature* Wales, UK 69 C6

Caribbean Sea Atlantic Ocean 34-35

Carlisle England, UK 68 D4

Carlsbad New Mexico, USA 26 D3

Carlsberg Ridge *Undersea feature* Indian Ocean 112 B3

Carnarvon Australia 128 A4

Carnegie, Lake *Lake* Australia 129 C5

Carolina Brazil 41 F3

Caroline Island *Island* Kiribati 127 H3

Caroline Islands *Island group* Micronesia 126 B1

Caroní *River* Venezuela 39 F2

Carpathian Mountains *Mountain range* E Europe *var.* Carpathians 61 E4

Carpathians *see* Carpathian Mountains

Carpaţii Meridionali *Mountain range* Romania *Eng.* South Carpathians, Transylvanian Alps 88 B4

Carpentaria, Gulf of *Sea feature* Australia 126 A4

Carson City Nevada, USA 25 C5

Cartagena Colombia 38 B1

Cartagena Spain 73 F3

Cartago Costa Rica 33 E4

Cartwright Canada 19 G2

Carúpano Venezuela 39 E1

Casablanca Morocco 50 C2

Casa Grande Arizona, USA 26 3

Cascade Range *Mountain range* Canada/USA 24 B3

Cascais Portugal 72 B4

Caseyr, Raas *Coastal feature* Somalia 48 E4

Casper Wyoming, USA 22 C3

Caspian Sea *Inland sea* Asia/Europe 94 A4

Castellón de la Plana Spain 73 F3

Castelo Branco Portugal 72 C3

Castries *Capital of* St Lucia 35 G4

Castro Chile 45 B6

Cat Island *Island* Bahamas 34 D1

Catania Italy 77 D7

Catanzaro Italy 77 D6

Cauca *River* Colombia 38 B2

Caucasus *Mountains* Asia/Europe 61 G4 92 B3

Cauquenes Chile 44 B4

Caura *River* Venezuela 39 E2

Caviana, Ilha *Island* Brazil 41 F1

Cawnpore *see* Kānpur

Caxias do Sul Brazil 42 D4

Cayenne *Capital of* French Guiana 39 H3

Cayman Islands *External territory* UK, West Indies 34

Cayman Trench *Undersea feature* Caribbean Sea 34 B3

Cebu Philippines 121 E2

Cedar Rapids Iowa, USA 23 G3

Cedros, Isla *Island* Mexico 30 A2

Cefalù Italy 77 C7

Celebes *see* Sulawesi

Celebes Sea Pacific Ocean *Ind.* Laut Sulawesi 122 B3

Celje Slovenia 80 A2

Central African Republic *Country* C Africa *abbrev.* CAR 56-57

Central Makrān Range *Mountains* Pakistan 114 A3

Central Russian Upland Russian Federation 92 B3

Central Siberian Plateau *Plateau* Russian Federation 95 E3

Cephalonia *see* Kefallonía

Cernăuţi *see* Chernivtsi

Cēsis Latvia *Ger.* Wenden 86 C3

České Budějovice Czech Republic *Ger.* Budweis 79 B5

Ceuta *External territory* Spain, N Africa 50 C1

Cévennes *Mountains* France 71 C6

Ceylon *see* Sri Lanka

Ceylon Plain *Undersea feature* Indian Ocean 117 F4

Chad *Country* C Africa 56

Chad, Lake *Lake* C Africa 48 C4

Chāgai Hills *Mountains* Pakistan 114 A2

Chalándri Greece 85 C5

Chalkída Greece 85 C5

Châlons-sur-Marne France 70 D3

Chambéry France 71 D5

Champlaim Seamount *Undersea feature* Atlantic Ocean 43 G1

Chañaral Chile 44 B2

Chandīgarh India 114 D2

Chang, Ko *Island* Thailand 119 C5

Changchun China 108 D3

Chang Jiang *River* China *var.* Yangtze 104 D4 109 B5

Changsha China 109 C6

Changzhi China 109 C5

Chaniá Greece 85 C7

Channel Islands *Islands* UK 69 D8

Channel-Port-aux-Basques Canada 19 G4

Channel Tunnel France/UK 69 E7

Chapala, Lago de *Lake* Mexico 30 D4

Chardzhev Turkmenistan *prev.* Chardzhou, *prev.* Leninsk, *Turkm.* Chärjew 102 D3

Chardzhou *see* Chardzhev

Chari *River* C Africa 56 C3

Chārīkār Afghanistan 103 E4

Chärjew *see* Chardzhev

Charleroi Belgium 67 C7

Charleston South Carolina, USA 29 F2

Charleston West Virginia, USA 20 D5

Charleville Australia 130 B2
Charlotte North Carolina, USA 29 F2
Charlotte Amalie *Capital of* Virgin Islands 35 F3
Charlottesville Virginia, USA 21 E5
Charlottetown Canada 19 G4
Chartres France 70 C3
Châteauroux France 70 C4
Chatham Islands *Islands* New Zealand 122 D4
Chattanooga Tennessee, USA 28 D2
Chauk Myanmar 118 A3
Chaves Portugal 72 C2
Cheboksary Russian Federation 91 C5
Cheboygan Michigan, USA 20 C2
Cheju-do *Island* South Korea 109 E5
Cheju Strait *Sea feature* South Korea 109 E5
Cheleken Turkmenistan 102 E2
Chelyabinsk Russian Federation 94 C3
Chemnitz Germany *prev.* Karl-Marx-Stadt 75 D5
Chenāb *River* Pakistan 114 C2
Chengdu China 109 B5
Cherbourg France 70 B3
Cherepovets Russian Federation 90 B4
Cherkasy Ukraine 89 E2
Cherkessk Russian Federation 91 A7
Chernigov *see* Chernihiv
Chernihiv Ukraine *Rus.* Chernigov 89 E1
Chernivtsi Ukraine *Rus.* Chernovtsy, *Rom.* Cernăuţi 88 C3
Chernobyl' *see* Chornobyl'
Chernovtsy *see* Chernivtsi
Chernyakhovsk Kaliningrad, Russian Federation 86 A4
Cherskiy Range *Mountains* Russian Federation 93 G2
Chesapeake Bay *Sea feature* USA 21 F5
Chester England, UK 69 D5
Cheyenne Wyoming, USA 22 D4

Chiang Mai Thailand 118 B4
Chiba Japan 111 D5
Chicago Illinois, USA 20 B3
Chichigalpa Nicaragua 32 C3
Chiclayo Peru 40 A3
Chicoutimi Canada 19 E4
Chidley, Cape *Coastal feature* Canada 19 E1
Chiemsee *Lake* Germany 75 C7
Chifeng China 107 G2
Chihuahua Mexico 30 C2
Chile *Country* S South America 44-45
Chilean Claim in Antarctica 132 B2
Chile Basin *Undersea feature* Pacific Ocean 123 G4
Chile Chico Chile 45 B6
Chillán Chile 44 B4
Chiloé, Isla de *Island* Chile 45 B6
Chimborazo *Peak* Ecuador 36 B7
Chimbote Peru 40 A3
Chimkent *see* Shymkent
Chimoio Mozambique 59 E3
China *Country* E Asia 106-107 108-109
Chindwin *River* Myanmar 118 A2
Chingola Zambia 58 D2
Chíos Greece 85 D5
Chíos *Island* Greece *prev.* Khíos 85 D5
Chirchik Uzbekistan *Uzb.* Chirchiq 103 E2
Chirchiq *see* Chirchik
Chiriquí, Golfo de *Sea feature* Panama 33 E5
Chişinău *Capital of* Moldova, *var.* Kishinev 88 D3
Chita Russian Federation 95 F4
Chitré Panama 33 F5
Chittagong Bangladesh 115 G4
Chitungwiza Zimbabwe 58 D3
Chojnice Poland 78 C3
Choluteca Honduras 32 C3
Choma Zambia 58 D2
Chomutov Czech Republic *Ger.* Komotau 78 A4
Chon Buri Thailand 119 C5
Ch'ŏngjin North Korea 108 E3

Chongqing China *var.* Chungking 109 B6
Chonos, Archipiélago de los *Island group* Chile 45 B6
Chornobyl' Ukraine *Rus.* Chernobyl' 89 E1
Choybalsan Mongolia 107 F2
Christchurch New Zealand 131 G4
Christmas Island *External territory* Australia, Indian Ocean 112 D4
Christmas Island *see* Kiritimati
Chubut *River* Argentina 45 B6
Chudskoye Ozero *see* Peipus, Lake
Chuí Brazil *var.* Chuy 42 C5
Chukchi Sea Arctic Ocean *Rus.* Chukotskoye More 12 C1
Chukotskoye More *see* Chukchi Sea
Chumphon Thailand 119 C6
Chungking *see* Chongqing
Chuquicamata Chile 44 B2
Chur Switzerland 75 B7
Churchill Canada 17 G4
Churchill Falls Canada 19 F3
Chuuk Islands *Island group* Micronesia 126 B1
Chuy *see* Chuí
Cienfuegos Cuba 34 B2
Cieza Spain 73 F4
Cincinnati Ohio, USA 20 C4
Cirebon Indonesia 120 C5
Citlaltépetl *Peak* Mexico *var.* Pico de Orizaba 115 E5
Ciudad Bolívar Venezuela 39 E2
Ciudad del Este Paraguay 42 C3
Ciudad de México *see* Mexico City
Ciudad Guayana Venezuela 39 E2
Ciudad Juárez Mexico 30 C1
Ciudad Obregón Mexico 30 B2
Ciudad Ojeda Venezuela 38 C1
Ciudad Real Spain 73 E4
Ciudad Victoria Mexico 31 E3
Clarenville Canada 19 H3
Clarksville Tennessee, USA 28 D1
Clearwater Florida, USA 29 E4

Clermont-Ferrand France 71 C5

Cleveland Ohio, USA 20 D3

Clipperton Island *External territory* France, Pacific Ocean 123 F3

Cloncurry Australia 126 B5 130 A1

Clovis New Mexico, USA 27 E2

Cluj-Napoca Romania 88 B3

Coast Mountains *Mountain range* Canada 14 C2

Coast Ranges *Mountain range* W USA 24 A3

Coats Island *Island* Canada 18 C1

Coatzacoalcos Mexico 31 G4

Cobán Guatemala 32 B2

Cochabamba Bolivia 40 C4

Cochin India 116 D3

Cochrane Canada 18 C4

Cochrane Chile 45 B6

Coco *River* Honduras/Nicaragua 32 D2

Cocos (Keeling) Islands *External territory* Australia, Indian Ocean 112 D4

Cod, Cape *Coastal feature* NE USA 15 F3 21 G3

Coeur d'Alene Idaho, USA 24 C2

Coffs Harbour Australia 130 C2

Coihaique Chile 45 B6

Coimbatore India 116 D3

Coimbra Portugal 72 C3

Colbeck, Cape *Coastal feature* Antarctica 132 C4

Colchester England, UK 69 E6

Colhué Huapi, Lago *Lake* Argentina 45 B6

Colima *Peak* Mexico 15 E5

Colmar France 70 E4

Cologne *see* Köln

Colombia *Country* N South America 38-39

Colombian Basin *Undersea feature* Caribbean Sea 34 D5

Colombo *Capital of* Sri Lanka 117 E3

Colón, Archipiélago de *see* Galapagos Islands

Colorado *State* USA 22 C5

Colorado *River* USA 14 D3

Colorado *River* Argentina 45 C5

Colorado Plateau *Upland region* S USA 26 B1

Colorado Springs Colorado, USA 22 D4

Columbia South Carolina, USA 29 F2

Columbia *River* NW USA 24 C1

Columbus Georgia, USA 28 D3

Columbus Mississippi, USA 28 C2

Columbus Nebraska, USA 23 E4

Columbus Ohio, USA 20 D4

Comayagua Honduras 32 C2

Comilla Bangladesh 115 G4

Communism Peak *Peak* Tajikistan *Rus.* Pik Kommunizma, *prev.* Stalin Peak, Garmo Peak 92 C4

Como, Lago di *Lake* Italy 76 B2

Comodoro Rivadavia Argentina 45 C6

Comoros *Country* Indian Ocean 59

Conakry *Capital of* Guinea 52 C4

Concepción Chile 45 B5

Concepción Paraguay 42 B2

Conchos *River* Mexico 30 C2

Concord California, USA 25 B6

Concord New Hampshire, USA 20 G2

Concordia E Argentina 44 D3

Congo *Country* C Africa 57

Congo *River* C Africa *var.* Zaire 49 C5

Congo Basin *Drainage basin* C Africa 49 C5

Connecticut *State* USA 21 G3

Constance, Lake *River* C Europe 75 B7

Constantine Algeria 51 E1

Constantinople *see* İstanbul

Constanța Romania 88 D5

Coober Pedy Australia 129 E5

Cook, Mount New Zealand *prev.* Aorangi 125 E5

Cook Islands *External territory* New Zealand, Pacific Ocean 122 D4

Cook Strait *Sea feature* New Zealand 131 G3

Cooktown Australia 126 B4

Coos Bay Oregon, USA 24 A3

Copenhagen *Capital of* Denmark 65 B7

Copiapó Chile 44 B3

Coppermine Canada 17 E3

Coquimbo Chile 44 B3

Corabia Romania 88 B5

Coral Sea Pacific Ocean 122 C3

Coral Sea Islands *External territory* Australia, Coral Sea 126 C4

Corantijn *River* Guyana/Suriname *var.* Courantyne 39 C3

Cordillera Cantábrica *Mountain range* Spain 72 D1

Córdoba Argentina 44 C3

Córdoba Spain 72 D4

Cordova Alaska, USA 16 D3

Corfu *see* Kérkyra

Corinth *see* Kórinthos

Corinth, Gulf of *see* Korinthiakós Kólpos

Corinto Nicaragua 32 C3

Cork Ireland 69 A6

Corner Brook Canada 19 G3

Coro Venezuela 38 D1

Coromandel New Zealand 131 G2

Coronel Oviedo Paraguay 42 C2

Corpus Christi Texas, USA 27 G4

Corrib, Lough *Lake* Ireland 69 A5

Corrientes Argentina 44 D3

Corse *Island* France *Eng.* Corsica 71 E7 82 D2

Corsica *see* Corse

Çorum Turkey 96 D2

Corvallis Oregon, USA 24 A3

Cosenza Italy 77 D6

Costa Blanca *Coastal region* Spain 73 F4

Costa Brava *Coastal region* Spain 73 H2

Costa Rica *Country* Central America 32-33

Côte d'Ivoire *see* Ivory Coast

Cotonou Benin 53 F5

Cotopaxi *Peak* Ecuador 36 B2

Cottbus Germany 74 D4

Council Bluffs Iowa, USA 23 F4

Courantyne *River* Guyana/Suriname *var.* Corantijn 39 G3

Courland Lagoon *Sea feature* Baltic Sea 86 A4

Coventry England, UK 69 D6

Covilhã Portugal 72 C3

Cozumel, Isla de *Island* Mexico 31 H3

Cracow *see* Kraków

Craiova Romania 88 B5

Cremona Italy 76 B2

Cres *Island* Croatia 80 A3

Crescent City California, USA 24 A4

Crete Greece *see* Kríti 83 F4

Crete, Sea of Mediterranean Sea *Gk.* Kritikó Pélagos 85 D5

Crimea *Peninsula* Ukraine *var.* Krym 88 F3

Croatia *Country* SE Europe 80

Croker Island *Island* Australia 128 D2

Crotone Italy 77 E6

Crozet Basin *Undersea feature* Indian Ocean 113 B6

Crozet Islands *Island group* Indian Ocean 113 B6

Cruzeiro do Sul Brazil 40 B3

Cuanza *River* Angola 58 B1

Cuba *Country* West Indies 34

Cubango *see* Okavango

Cúcuta Colombia 38 C2

Cuenca Ecuador 38 A5

Cuenca Spain 73 E3

Cuernavaca Mexico 31 E4

Cuiabá Brazil 41 E4

Cuito *River* Angola 58 C2

Culiacán Mexico 30 C3

Cumaná Venezuela 39 E1

Cumberland Maryland, USA 21 E4

Cumberland *River* C USA 20 C5

Cunene *River* Angola/Namibia 58 B2

Cunnamulla Australia 130 B2

Curicó Chile 44 B4

Curitiba Brazil 42 D3

Cusco Peru *prev.* Cuzco 40 B4

Cuttack India 115 F5

Cuxhaven Germany 74 B3

Cuyuni *River* Guyana/Venezuela 39 F2

Cuzco *see* Cusco

Cyclades *see* Kykládes

Cymru *see* Wales

Cyprus *Country* Mediterranean Sea 96 C5

Czechoslovakia *see* Czech Republic *or* Slovakia

Czech Republic *Country* C Europe 78-79

Częstochowa Poland *Ger.* Tschenstochau 78 C4

D

Dacca *see* Dhaka

Dagden *see* Hiiumaa

Dagö *see* Hiiumaa

Dagupan Philippines 121 E1

Da Hinggan Ling *Mountain range* China *Eng.* Great Khingan Range 107 G1

Dahomey *see* Benin

Dakar *Capital of* Senegal 52 B3

Đakovo Croatia 80 C3

Dalaman Turkey 96 B4

Đa Lat Vietnam 119 E5

Dali China 109 A6

Dalian China 108 D4

Dallas Texas, USA 27 G3

Dalmacija *Region* Croatia 80 B4

Daloa Ivory Coast 52 D5

Daly Waters Australia 128 E3

Damān India 114 C5

Damas *see* Damascus

Damascus Syria *var.* Esh Sham, *Fr.* Damas, *Ar.* Dimashq 98 B4

Dampier Australia 128 B4

Đa Năng Vietnam 119 E4

Daneborg Greenland 63 E3

Dangara Tajikistan 103 E3

Danmark Greenland 63 E2

Danmarksstraedet *see* Denmark Strait

Danube *River* C Europe 60 D4

Danube Delta *Wetland* Romania/Ukraine 88 D5

Danville Virginia, USA 21 E5

Danzig *see* Gdańsk

Dar'ā Syria 99 B5

Dardanelles *Sea feature* Turkey *Turk.* Çanakkale Boğazı 96 A2

Dar es Salaam Tanzania 55 C8

Darhan Mongolia 107 E2

Darien, Gulf of *Sea feature* Caribbean Sea 33 G5

Darling *River* Australia 130 B2

Darmstadt Germany 75 B5

Darnah Libya 51 H2

Darnley, Cape *Coastal feature* Antarctica 133 G2

Dartmoor *Region* England, UK 69 C7

Dartmouth Canada 19 G4

Darwin Australia 128 D2

Dashhowuz *see* Dashkhovuz

Dashkhovuz Turkmenistan *prev.* Tashauz, *Turkm.* Dashhowuz 102 C2

Datong China 108 C4

Daugava *see* Western Dvina

Daugavpils Latvia *Ger.* Dünaburg, *Rus.* Dvinsk 86 C4

Dāvangere India 116 D2

Davao Philippines 121 F2

Davenport Iowa, USA 23 G3

David Panama 33 E5

Davis Sea Indian Ocean 133 H3

Davis Strait *Sea feature* Atlantic Ocean 17 H2 62 B4

Dawson Canada 16 D3

Dayr az Zawr Syria 98 D3

Dayton Ohio, USA 20 C4

Daytona Beach Florida, USA 29 F4

Dead Sea *Salt Lake* SW Asia *Ar.* Al Baḥr al Mayyit, Baḥrat Lūṭ, *Heb.* Yam HaMelaḥ 99 B5

Death Valley *Valley* W USA 14 D4 25 D6

Debre Zeyit Ethiopia 55 C5

Debrecen Hungary *prev.* Debreczen, *Ger.* Debreczin 79 D6

Debreczen *see* Debrecen

Debreczin *see* Debrecen

Decatur Illinois, USA 20 B4

Deccan *Plateau* India 104 B3

Děčín Czech Republic *Ger.* Tetschen 78 B4

Dej Romania 88 B3

Delaware *State* USA 21 F4

Delaware Bay *Sea feature* USA 21 F4

Delémont Switzerland 75 A7

Delft Netherlands 66 B4

Delfzijl Netherlands 66 E1

Delhi India 114 D3

Del Rio Texas, USA 27 F4

Demchok *Disputed region*
China/India *var.* Dêmqog 106
A4 115 E2

Dêmqog *see* Demchok

Denali *Peak* Alaska, USA
prev. Mount McKinley 14 C2

Den Helder Netherlands 66 C2

Denizli Turkey 96 B4

Denmark *Country* NW
Europe 65

Denmark Strait *Sea feature*
Greenland/Iceland *var.*
Danmarksstraedet 63 D3

Denpasar Indonesia 120 D5

Denton Texas, USA 27 G2

Denver Colorado, USA 22 D4

Dera Ghāzi Khān Pakistan
114 C2

Dera Ismāīl Khān Pakistan
114 C2

Derby England, UK 69 D6

Derg, Lough *Lake* Ireland 69 B6

Desē Ethiopia 54 C4

Deseado *River* Argentina
45 C6

Des Moines Iowa, USA 23 F3

Despoto Planina *see* Rhodope
Mountains

Dessau Germany 74 C4

Desventurados, Islas de los
Islands Chile 37 A5 123 G4

Detroit Michigan, USA 20 D3

Deutschendorf *see* Poprad

Deva Romania 88 B4

Deventer Netherlands 66 D3

Devollit, Lumi i *River* Albania
81 D6

Devon Island *Island* Canada
17 G2

Devonport Tasmania, Australia
130 B5

Dezfūl Iran 100 C3

Dhaka *Capital of* Bangladesh
var. Dacca 115 G4

Dhanbād India 115 F4

Dhanushkodi India 116 D3

Dhrepanon, Ákra *Coastal feature*
Greece 84 C4

Diamantina *River* Australia
130 B1

Dickinson North Dakota, USA
22 D2

Diekirch Luxembourg 67 D7

Dieppe France 70 C3

Diffa Niger 53 H3

Digul *River* Indonesia 121 H5

Dijon France 70 D4

Dīla Ethiopia 55 C5

Dili Indonesia 121 F5

Dilling Sudan 54 B4

Dilolo Zaire 57 D8

Dimashq *see* Damascus

Dimitrovo *see* Pernik

Dinant Belgium 67 C7

Dinara *Mountains* Bosnia &
Herzegovina/Croatia 80 B4

Dingle Bay *Sea feature* Ireland
69 A5

Diourbel Senegal 52 B3

Dirē Dawa Ethiopia 55 D5

Dirk Hartog Island *Island*
Australia 129 A5

Disappointment, Lake *Salt lake*
Australia 118 C4

Dispur India 115 G3

Divinópolis Brazil 43 F1

Diyarbakır Turkey 97 E4

Djambala Congo 57 B6

Djibouti *Country* E Africa 54

Djibouti *Capital of* Djibouti
var. Jibuti 54 D4

Djúpivogur Iceland 63 E4

Dnieper *River* E Europe 51 F4

Dniester *River*
Moldova/Ukraine 88 D3

Dnipropetrovs'k Ukraine
89 F3

Dobele Latvia *Ger.* Doblen
86 B3

Doblen *see* Dobele

Doboj Bosnia & Herzegovina
80 C3

Dobrich Bulgaria 84 E1

Dodecanese *see* Dodekánisos

Dodekánisos *Islands* Greece
Eng. Dodecanese 85 E6

Dodge City Kansas, USA 23 E5

Dodoma *Capital of* Tanzania
55 C7

Doğu Karadeniz Dağları
Mountains Turkey
var. Anadolu Dağları 97 E2

Doha *Capital of* Qatar
Ar. Ad Dawḩah 101 C5

Dolomites *see* Dolomiti

Dolomiti *Mountains* Italy
Eng. Dolomites 76 C2

Dolores Argentina 44 D4

Dominica *Country* West
Indies 35

Dominican Republic *Country*
West Indies 35

Don *River* Russian Federation
94 A3

Donegal Bay *Sea feature* Ireland
69 A5

Donets *River* Russian
Federation/Ukraine 88 G3
91 A6

Donets'k Ukraine 89 G3

Dongola Sudan 54 B3

Dongting Hu *Lake* China
109 C6

Donostia *see* San Sebastián

Dordogne *River* France
71 B5

Dordrecht Netherlands 66 C4

Dornbirn Austria 75 B7

Dorpat *see* Tartu

Dortmund Germany 74 A4

Dosso Niger 53 F3

Dothan Alabama, USA 28 D3

Douai France 70 C2

Douala Cameroon 57 A5

Douglas UK 69 C5

Douglas Arizona, USA 26 C3

Dourados Brazil 42 C2

Douro *River* Portugal/Spain
Sp. Duero 72 C2

Dover England, UK 69 E7

Dover Delaware, USA 21 F4

Dōzen *Island* Japan 111 B5

Drakensberg *Mountain range*
Lesotho/South Africa
58 D5

Drake Passage *Sea feature*
Atlantic Ocean/Pacific Ocean
37 C8

Dráma Greece 84 C3

Drammen Norway 65 B6

Drau *River* C Europe *var.* Drava
75 D7 80 C3

Drava *River* C Europe *var.* Drau
79 C7

Dresden Germany 74 D4

Drina *River* Bosnia &
Herzegovina/Yugoslavia
80 D4

Gold Coast *Coastal region*
Australia 130 D2

Goldingen *see* Kuldīga

Golmud China 106 D4

Goma Zaire 57 E6

Gomel' *see* Homyel'

Gómez Palacio Mexico 30 D2

Gonaïves Haiti 34 D3

Gonder Ethiopia 54 C4

Good Hope, Cape of *Coastal feature* South Africa 58 C5

Goondiwindi Australia 130 C2

Goose Lake *Lake* W USA 24 B4

Goré Chad 56 C4

Gorē Ethiopia 55 C5

Gorgān Iran 100 D3

Gorki *see* Horki

Gor'kiy *see* Nizhniy Novgorod

Gorlovka *see* Horlivka

Gorontalo Indonesia 121 E4

Gorzów Wielkopolski Poland
Ger. Landsberg 78 B3

Gospić Croatia 80 A3

Gostivar Macedonia 81 D5

Göteborg Sweden 65 B7

Gotland *Island* Sweden 65 C7

Gotō-rettō *Island group* Japan
111 A6

Göttingen Germany 74 B4

Gouda Netherlands 66 C4

Gough Island *External territory*
UK, Atlantic Ocean 47 D6

Gouin, Réservoir *Reservoir*
Canada 18 D4

Governador Valadares Brazil
41 G4 43 F1

Gozo *Island* Malta 77 C8

Gračanica Bosnia & Herzegovina
80 C3

Grafton Australia 130 D2

Graham Land *Region* Antarctica
132 B3

Grampian Mountains *Mountains*
Scotland, UK 68 C3

Granada Nicaragua 32 D3

Granada Spain 73 E4

Gran Canaria *Island* Spain
50 A3

Gran Chaco *Region* C South
America 36 C4

Grand Bahama *Island* Bahamas
34 C1

Grand Banks *Undersea feature*
Atlantic Ocean 46 B3

Grand Canyon *Valley* SW USA
26 B1

Grande, Bahía *Sea feature*
Argentina 37 C7

Grande, Rio *River* Brazil 42 D4
43 E1

Grande Comore *Island* Comoros
59 F2

Grande Prairie Canada 17 E5

Grand Erg Occidental *Desert region* Algeria 50 D2

Grand Erg Oriental *Desert region*
Algeria/Tunisia 51 E3

Grand Falls Canada 19 H3

Grand Forks North Dakota, USA
23 E1

Grand Junction Colorado, USA
22 C4

Grand Rapids Michigan, USA
20 C3

Graudenz *see* Grudziądz

Graz Austria 75 E7

Great Abaco *Island* Bahamas
34 C1

Great Ararat *see* Ararat, Mount

Great Australian Bight *Sea feature* Australia 122 B4
129 D6

Great Bahama Bank *Undersea feature* Atlantic Ocean 34 C2

Great Barrier Reef *Coral reef*
Coral Sea 122 C4

Great Basin *Region* USA 24 D4

Great Bear Lake *Lake* Canada
17 E3

Great Dividing Range *Mountain range* Australia 124 D3

Greater Antarctica *Region*
Antarctica 133 F3

Greater Antilles *Island group*
West Indies 34 C3

Great Exuma Island *Island*
Bahamas 34 C2

Great Falls Montana, USA 22 B1

Great Inagua *Island* Bahamas
34 D2

Great Khingan Range *see*
Da Hinggan Ling

Great Lakes, The *Lakes*
N America *see* Erie, Huron,
Michigan, Ontario, Superior
15 F3

Great Nicobar *Island* India
117 H3

Great Plain of China *Region*
China 104 D2

Great Plains *Region* N America
14 D3

Great Rift Valley *Valley*
E Africa/SW Asia 55 C6

Great Salt Lake *Salt lake* Utah,
USA 22 B3

Great Sand Sea *Desert region*
Egypt/Libya 51 H3

Great Sandy Desert *Desert*
Australia 128 C4

Great Sandy Desert *see*
Rub' al Khali

Great Slave Lake *Lake* Canada
17 F4

Great Victoria Desert *Desert*
Australia 129 C5

Gredos, Sierra de *Mountains*
Spain 72 D3

Greece *Country* SE Europe 84-85

Green Bay Wisconsin, USA
20 B2

Greenland *External territory*
Denmark, Atlantic Ocean
var. Grønland 62

Greenland Basin *Undersea feature*
Atlantic Ocean 63 F2

Greenland Sea Atlantic Ocean
63 F2

Greenock Scotland, UK
68 C4

Greensboro North Carolina,
USA 29 F1

Greenville South Carolina, USA
29 E2

Greifswald Germany 74 D2

Grenada *Country* West Indies
35 G5

Grenoble France 71 D5

Greymouth New Zealand
131 F3

Grimsby England, UK 69 E5

Grodno *see* Hrodna

Groningen Netherlands 66 E1

Grønland *see* Greenland

Grootfontein Namibia 58 C3

Grosseto Italy 76 B4

Grosskanizsa *see* Nagykanizsa

Groznyy Russian Federation 91
B7 94 A4

Grudziądz Poland
Ger. Graudenz 78 C3

Grünberg in Schlesien *see*
Zielona Góra

Guadalajara Mexico 30 D4

Hattiesburg Mississippi, USA
28 C3

Hat Yai Thailand 119 C7

Haugesund Norway 65 A6

Havana Capital of Cuba
Sp. La Habana 34 B2

Havre Montana, USA 22 C1

Havre-Saint-Pierre Canada
19 F3

Hawaii State USA 123 E2

Hawaiian Islands Islands USA
93 H4

Hawler see Arbīl

Hawthorne Nevada, USA 25 C6

Hay River Canada 17 E4

Hays Kansas, USA 23 E4

Heard Island Island Indian
Ocean 113 C7

Heerenveen Netherlands 66 D2

Heerlen Netherlands 67 D6

Ḥefa Israel prev. Haifa 99 A5

Hefei China 109 D5

Heidelberg Germany 75 B6

Heilbronn Germany 75 B6

Helena Montana, USA 22 B2

Helmand River Afghanistan
102 C5

Helmond Netherlands 67 D5

Helsingborg Sweden 65 B7

Helsingør Denmark 65 B7

Helsinki Capital of Finland
65 D6

Ḥelwân Egypt 54 B1

Hengelo Netherlands 66 E3

Henzada Myanmar 118 A4

Herāt Afghanistan 102 C4

Hermansverk Norway 65 A5

Hermosillo Mexico 30 B2

Herning Denmark 65 A7

Hialeah Florida, USA 29 F5

Hiiumaa Island Estonia
Ger. Dagden, Swed. Dagö
86 C2

Hildesheim Germany 74 B4

Hilla see Al Ḥillah

Hilversum Netherlands 66 C3

Himalayas Mountain range
S Asia 104 B2

Himora Ethiopia 54 C4

Ḥimṣ Syria 98 B3

Hindu Kush Mountain range
C Asia 103 E4

Hiroshima Japan 111 B5

Hitachi Japan 110 D4

Hjørring Denmark 65 A7

Hlybokaye Belarus
Rus. Glubokoye 87 D5

Hobart Tasmania 130 B5

Hobbs New Mexico, USA
5627 E3

Hồ Chi Minh Vietnam var. Ho
Chi Minh City, prev. Saigon
119 E6

Ho Chi Minh City see Hồ Chi
Minh

Hodeida see Al Ḥudaydah

Hoek van Holland Netherlands
66 B4

Hoggar see Ahaggar

Hohhot China 107 F3

Hokkaidō Island Japan 110 D2

Holguín Cuba 34 C2

Hollywood Florida, USA 29 F5

Holland see Netherlands

Holon Israel 99 A5

Ilolyhead Wales, UK 69 C5

Homyel' Belarus Rus. Gomel'
87 D7

Honduras Country Central
America 32-33

Honduras, Gulf of Sea feature
Caribbean Sea 32 C2

Hønefoss Norway 65 B6

Hồng Gai Vietnam 118 E3

Hong Kong External territory
UK, E Asia 109 C7

Hongze Hu Lake China 109 D5

Honiara Capital of Solomon
Islands 126 C3

Honolulu Hawaii, USA 123 E2

Honshū Island Japan 110 D3

Honshu Ridge Undersea feature
Pacific Ocean 105 F2

Hoorn Netherlands 66 C2

Hopa Turkey 97 F2

Hopedale Canada 19 F2

Hopkinsville Kentucky, USA
20 B5

Horki Belarus Rus. Gorki
87 E6

Horlivka Ukraine Rus. Gorlovka
88 G3

Horn, Cape Coastal feature Chile
45 C8

Hórog see Khorog

Horsens Denmark 65 A7

Hotan China 106 B4

Hot Springs Arkansas, USA
28 B2

Hotspur Seamount Undersea
feature Atlantic Ocean 41 H5
43 H1

Houston Texas, USA 27 G4

Hovd Mongolia 106 C2

Hövsgöl Nuur Lake Mongolia
106 D1

Howe, Cape Coastal feature
Australia 124 D3 130 C4

Hradec Králové Czech Republic
Ger. Königgrätz 79 B5

Hrodna Belarus Rus. Grodno
87 B5

Huacho Peru 40 A3

Huainan China 109 D5

Huambo Angola 58 B2

Huancayo Peru 40 B4

Huang He River China
Eng. Yellow River 104 D2
107 F4 108 C4

Huánuco Peru 40 B4

Huaraz Peru 40 B3

Huascarán Peak Peru 36 B3

Hubli India 116 C2

Hudson River NE USA 21 F3

Hudson Bay Sea feature Canada
15 E2

Hudson Strait Sea feature
Canada 15 F2

Huế Vietnam 118 E4

Huehuetenango Guatemala
32 B2

Huelva Spain 72 C4

Huesca Spain 73 F2

Hughenden Australia 130 B1

Hull see Kingston upon Hull

Hulun Nur Lake China 107 F1

Humboldt River W USA 25 C5

Hungarian Plain Plain C Europe
83 E1

Hungary Country C Europe 79

Huntington West Virginia, USA
20 D5

Huntsville Alabama, USA
28 D2

Hurghada Egypt 54 B2

Huron, Lake Lake Canada/USA
15 F3

Ittoqqortoormiit Greenland 13 B7 63 B3
Iturup *Island* Japan/Russian Federation (disputed) 110 E1
Ivanhoe Australia 130 B3
Ivano-Frankivs'k Ukraine 88 C2
Ivanovo Russian Federation 90 B4
Ivittuut Greenland 62 B4
Ivory Coast *Country* W Africa *Fr.* Côte d'Ivoire 52
Ivujivik Canada 18 D1
Iwaki Japan 110 D4
Izabal, Lago de *Lake* Guatemala 32 C2
Izhevsk Russian Federation 91 C5 94 B3
İzmir Turkey *prev.* Smyrna 96 A3
İzmit Turkey *var.* Kocaeli 96 B2
Izu-shotō *Island group* Japan 111 D6

J

Jabalpur India 114 E4
Jackson Mississippi, USA 28 C3
Jacksonville Florida, USA 29 E3
Jacksonville Texas, USA 27 G3
Jacmel Haiti 34 D3
Jaén Spain 73 E4
Jaffna Sri Lanka 117 E3
Jaipur India 114 D3
Jajce Bosnia & Herzegovina 80 B3
Jakarta *Capital of* Indonesia 120 C5
Jakobstad Finland 64 D4
Jakobstadt *see* Jēkabpils
Jalālābād Afghanistan 103 E4
Jalal-Abad *see* Dzhalal-Abad
Jalandhar India 114 D2
Jalapa Mexico 31 F4
Jamaame Somalia 55 D6
Jamaica *Country* West Indies 34
Jamāpur Bangladesh 115 G4
Jambi Indonesia 120 B4
James Bay *Sea feature* Canada 18 C3
Jammu *Disputed region* India/Pakistan 114 D2

Jāmnagar India 114 B4
Jan Mayen *External territory* Norway, Arctic Ocean 46 A2 63 F3
Japan *Country* E Asia 110-111
Japan, Sea of Pacific Ocean 93 F4 110 B3
Japan Trench *Undersea feature* Pacific Ocean 122 C2
Järvenpää Finland 65 D5
Jarvis Island *External territory* USA, Pacific Ocean 127 G2
Jaseur Seamount *Undersea feature* Atlantic Ocean 43 H2
Java *Island* Indonesia 120 D5
Java Sea Pacific Ocean *var.* Laut Jawa 112 D4
Java Trench *Undersea feature* Indian Ocean 112 D4
Jawa, Laut *see* Java Sea
Jayapura Indonesia 121 H4
Jedda *see* Jiddah
Jefferson City Missouri, USA 23 G4
Jekabpils Latvia *Ger.* Jakobstadt 86 C4
Jelgava Latvia *Ger.* Mitau 86 C3
Jember Indonesia 120 D5
Jena Germany 75 C5
Jérémie Haiti 34 D3
Jerevan *see* Yerevan
Jerez de la Frontera Spain 72 D5
Jericho West Bank 99 B5
Jerid, Chott el *Salt lake* Africa 82 D4
Jersey *Island* Channel Islands 69 D8
Jerusalem *Capital of* Israel 99 B5
Jesenice Slovenia 80 A2
Jhelum Pakistan 114 C2
Jiamusi China 108 E2
Jibuti *see* Djibouti
Jiddah Saudi Arabia *Eng.* Jedda 101 A6
Jihlava Czech Republic *Ger.* Iglau 79 B5
Jilin China 108 E3
Jīma Ethiopia 55 C5
Jinan China 109 C4
Jingdezhen China 109 D6
Jining China 107 F2
Jinotega Nicaragua 32 D3
Jinsha Jiang *River* China 109 A6
Jisr ash Shughūr Syria 98 B2

Jixi China 108 E3
Jīzān Saudi Arabia 101 B6
João Pessoa Brazil 41 H3
Jodhpur India 114 C3
Joensuu Finland 65 E5
Johannesburg South Africa 58 D4
Johnson City Tennessee, USA 29 E1
Johor Bahru Malaysia 120 B3
Joinville Brazil 42 D3
Joliet Illinois, USA 20 B3
Jönköping Sweden 65 B7
Jonquière Canada 19 E4
Jordan *Country* SW Asia 98-99
Jordan *River* SW Asia 99 B5
Jos Nigeria 53 G4
Juan Fernandez, Islas *Islands* Chile 123 C4
Juàzeiro Brazil 41 G3
Juàzeiro do Norte Brazil 41 G3
Juba Sudan 55 B5
Júcar *River* Spain 73 E3
Judenburg Austria 75 D7
Juigalpa Nicaragua 32 D3
Juiz de Fora Brazil 41 G5 43 F2
Juneau Alaska, USA 16 D4
Junín Argentina 44 D4
Jura *Mountains* France/Switzerland 70 D4 75 A7
Jura *Island* Scotland, UK 68 B4
Jurbarkas Lithuania *Ger.* Jurburg, *var.* Georgenburg 86 B4
Jurburg *see* Jurbarkas
Juruá *River* Brazil/Peru 40 C2
Juticalpa Honduras 32 D2
Jutland *see* Jylland
Juventud, Isla de la *Island* Cuba 34 B2
Jylland *Peninsula* Denmark *Eng.* Jutland 65 A7
Jyväskylä Finland 65 D5

K

K2 *Peak* China/Pakistan *Eng.* Mount Godwin Austen 104 C2
Kaachka *see* Kaka
Kaakhka *see* Kaka

Kabale Uganda 55 B6
Kabalebo Reservoir *Reservoir* Suriname 39 G3
Kabinda Zaire 57 D7
Kābol *see* Kābul
Kābul *Capital of* Afghanistan *Per.* Kābol 103 E4
Kachch, Gulf of *Sea feature* Arabian Sea 114 B4
Kachch, Rann of *Wetland* India/Pakistan *var.* Rann of Kutch 114 B4
Kadugli Sudan 54 B4
Kaduna Nigeria 53 G4
Kaédi Mauritania 52 C3
Kâğıthane Turkey 96 B2
Kagoshima Japan 111 A6
Kahramanmaraş Turkey *var.* Marash, Maraş 96 D4
Kai, Kepulauan *Island group* Indonesia 120 A3
Kaikoura New Zealand 131 G3
Kainji Reservoir *Reservoir* Nigeria 53 F4
Kairouan Tunisia 51 E1
Kaitaia New Zealand 131 G1
Kajaani Finland 64 E4
Kaka Turkmenistan *prev.* Kaakhka, *var.* Kaachka 102 C3
Kakhovs'ke Vodoskhovyshche *Reservoir* Ukraine 89 F3
Kalahari Desert *Desert* southern Africa 58 C3
Kalamariá Greece 84 B3
Kalámata Greece 85 B6
Kalāt Afghanistan 102 D5
Kalemie Zaire 57 E7
Kalgoorlie Australia 129 C6
Kaliningrad *External territory* Russian Federation 86 A4 94 A2
Kaliningrad Kaliningrad, Russian Federation *prev.* Königsberg 86 A4
Kalinkavichy Belarus *Rus.* Kalinkovichi 87 D7
Kalinkovichi *see* Kalinkavichy
Kalisch *see* Kalisz
Kalispell Montana, USA 22 B1
Kalisz Poland *Ger.* Kalisch 78 C4
Kalmar Sweden 65 C7

Kalpeni Island *Island* India 116 C3
Kama *River* Russian Federation 90 D4
Kamchatka *Peninsula* Russian Federation 95 A3
Kamchiya *River* Bulgaria 84 E2
Kamina Zaire 57 D7
Kamishli *see* Al Qāmishlī
Kamloops Canada 17 E5
Kampala *Capital of* Uganda 55 B6
Kâmpóng Cham Cambodia 119 D6
Kâmpóng Chhnăng Cambodia 119 D5
Kâmpóng Saôm Cambodia 119 D6
Kâmpôt Cambodia 119 D6
Kampuchea *see* Cambodia
Kam''yanets'-Podil's'kyy Ukraine 88 D3
Kananga Zaire 57 D7
Kanazawa Japan 110 C4
Kandahār Afghanistan *var.* Qandahār 102 D5
Kandi Benin 53 F4
Kandla India 114 C4
Kandy Sri Lanka 117 E3
Kanestron, Ákra *Coastal feature* Greece 84 C4
Kangaatsiaq Greenland 62 B4
Kangaroo Island *Island* Australia 124 C4
Kangerlussuaq Greenland 62 B4
Kangertittivaq *Region* Greenland 62 D3
Kanggye North Korea 108 E3
Kanjiža Yugoslavia 80 D2
Kankan Guinea 52 D4
Kano Nigeria 53 G4
Kānpur India *prev.* Cawnpore 115 E3
Kansas *State* USA 22-23
Kansas City Kansas, USA 23 F4
Kansas City Missouri, USA 23 F4
Kansk Russian Federation 95 E4
Kao-hsiung Taiwan 109 D7
Kaolack Senegal 52 B3
Kapchagay Kazakhstan 94 C5
Kapfenberg Austria 75 E7
Kaposvár Hungary 79 C7

Kapsukas *see* Marijampolė
Kapuas *River* Indonesia 120 C4
Kara-Balta Kyrgyzstan 103 F2
Kara-Bogaz-Gol, Zaliv *Sea feature* Caspian Sea 102 A2
Karabük Turkey 96 C2
Karāchi Pakistan 114 B4
Karaganda Kazakhstan 94 C4
Karaj Iran 100 C3
Karakol Kyrgyzstan *prev.* Przheval'sk 103 G2
Kara Kum *Desert* Turkmenistan *see* Karakumy 92 C4
Karakumskiy Kanal *Canal* Turkmenistan *Turkm.* Garagum Kanaly 102 C3
Karakumy *Desert* Turkmenistan *Turkm.* Garagum, *var.* Qara Qum *Eng.* Kara Kum 102 C2
Karamay China 106 B2
Karasburg Namibia 58 C4
Kara Sea *see* Karskoye More
Karbalā' Iraq *var.* Kerbala 100 B3
Kardítsa Greece 84 B4
Kariba, Lake *Lake* Zambia/Zimbabwe 58 D2
Karkinits'ka Zatoka *Sea feature* Black Sea 89 F4
Karl-Marx-Stadt *see* Chemnitz
Karlovac Croatia 80 B3
Karlovy Vary Czech Republic *Ger.* Karlsbad 79 A5
Karlsbad *see* Karlovy Vary
Karlskrona Sweden 65 C7
Karlsruhe Germany 75 B6
Karlstad Sweden 65 B6
Karnātaka *State* India 116 D1
Kárpathos *Island* Greece 85 E7
Kars Turkey 97 F2
Karshi Uzbekistan *prev.* Bek-Budi, *Uzb.* Qarshi 102 D3
Karskoye More Arctic Ocean *Eng.* Kara Sea 13 E6 90 E2 94 D2
Kasai *River* Zaire 57 C6
Kasama Zambia 59 E1
Kaschau *see* Košice
Kāshān Iran 100 C3
Kashi China 106 A3
Kashmir *Disputed region* India/Pakistan 114 D1
Kasongo Zaire 57 E6

Kassa *see* Košice

Kassala Sudan 54 C4

Kassel Germany 74 B4

Kastamonu Turkey 96 C2

Kateríni Greece 84 B4

Katha Myanmar 118 B2

Katherine Australia 128 D2

Kathmandu *Capital of* Nepal 115 F3

Katsina Nigeria 53 G3

Kauen *see* Kaunas

Kaunas Lithuania *Ger.* Kauen, *Pol.* Kowno, *Rus.* Kovno 86 B4

Kavadarci Macedonia 80 E5

Kavála Greece 84 C3

Kavaratti Island *Island* India 116 C3

Kawasaki Japan 111 D5

Kayan *River* Indonesia 120 D3

Kayes Mali 52 C3

Kayseri Turkey 96 D3

Kazakhskiy Melkosopochnik *see* Kazakh Upland

Kazakhstan *Country* C Asia 94

Kazakh Upland *Upland* Kazakhstan *var.* Kazakhskiy Melkosopochnik 92 D3

Kazan' Russian Federation 91 C5 94 B3

Kazandzhik *see* Gazandzhyk

Kazanlŭk Bulgaria 84 D2

Kéa Lithuania 86 B4

Kecskemét Hungary 79 D7

Kédainiai Lithuania 86 B4

Keetmanshoop Namibia 58 C4

Kefalloniá *Island* Greece *Eng.* Cephalonia 85 A5

Keith Australia 130 B4

Kelang Malaysia 120 B3

Kelmė Lithuania 86 B4

Kelowna Canada 17 E5

Kemerovo Russian Federation 94 D4

Kemi Finland 64 D4

Kemi *River* Finland 64 D3

Kemijärvi Finland 64 D3

Kendari Indonesia 121 E4

Kenema Sierra Leone 52 C4

Këneurgench Turkmenistan *prev.* Kunya-Urgench, *Turkm.* Köneürgench 102 C2

Kénitra Morocco 50 C2

Kennewick Washington, USA 24 C2

Kenora Canada 18 A3

Kentucky *State* USA 20 C5

Kenya *Country* E Africa 55

Kenya, Mount *see* Kirinyaga

Kerala *State* India 116 D3

Kerbala *see* Karbalā'

Kerch Ukraine 89 G4

Kerguelen Islands *Island group* Indian Ocean 113 C6

Kerguelen Plateau *Undersea feature* Indian Ocean 113 C7

Kerki Turkmenistan 102 D3

Kérkira *see* Kérkyra

Kérkyra Greece 84 A4

Kérkyra *Island* Greece *prev.* Kérkira, *Eng.* Corfu 84 A4

Kermadec Islands *Island group* Pacific Ocean 125 F3

Kermadec Trench *Undersea feature* Pacific Ocean 122 D4

Kerman Iran *var.* Kırman 100 D4

Kermánsháh *see* Bākhtarān

Kerora Eritrea 54 C3

Kerulen *River* China/Mongolia 107 E2

Ketchikan Alaska, USA 16 D4

Key West Florida, USA 29 E5

Khabarovsk Russian Federation 95 G4

Khanka, Lake *Lake* China/Russian Federation 108 E3

Khankendy *see* Xankändi

Kharkiv Ukraine *Rus.* Khar'kov 89 G2

Khartoum *Capital of* Sudan *var.* Al Khurṭūm 54 B4

Khartoum North Sudan 54 B4

Khāsh Iran 100 E4

Khaskovo Bulgaria 84 D2

Khaydarkan Kyrgyzstan *var.* Khaydarkan, Hajdarken 103 E2

Khaydarken *see* Khaydarkan

Kherson Ukraine 89 E4

Khíos *see* Chíos

Khmel'nyts'kyy Ukraine 88 C2

Khodzhent *see* Khudzhand

Khojend *see* Khudzhand

Khokand *see* Kokand

Kholm Afghanistan 103 E3

Khon Kaen Thailand 118 C4

Khorog Tajikistan *var.* Horog 103 F3

Khorramshahr Iran *var.* Khūnīnshahr 100 C4

Khouribga Morocco 50 C2

Khudzhand Tajikistan *prev.* Leninabad, Khodzhent, Khojend 103 E2

Khulna Bangladesh 115 G4

Khūnīnshahr *see* Khorramshahr

Khvoy Iran 100 B2

Kičevo Macedonia 81 D5

Kiel Germany 74 B2

Kielce Poland 78 D4

Kiev *Capital of* Ukraine *Ukr.* Kyyiv 89 E2

Kiffa Mauritania 52 C3

Kigali *Capital of* Rwanda 55 B6

Kigoma Tanzania 55 B7

Kikládhes *see* Kyklades

Kikwit Zaire 57 C7

Kilimanjaro *Peak* Tanzania 49 D5

Kilkís Greece 84 B3

Killarney Ireland 69 A6

Kimberley South Africa 58 D4

Kimberley Plateau *Upland* Australia 128 C3

Kindia Guinea 52 C4

Kindu Zaire 57 D6

King Island *Island* Australia 130 B4

Kingisepp *see* Kuressaare

Kingman Reef *External territory* USA, Pacific Ocean 127 G2

Kingston Canada 18 C5

Kingston *Capital of* Jamaica 34 C3

Kingston upon Hull England, UK *var.* Hull 69 D5

Kingstown St Vincent & The Grenadines 34 G4

King William Island *Island* Canada 17 F3

Kinneret, Yam *see* Tiberius, Lake

Kinshasa *Capital of* Zaire *prev.* Léopoldville 57 B6

Kirghizia *see* Kyrgyzstan

Kirghiz Steppe *Plain* Kazakhstan 95 B4

Kiribati *Country* Pacific Ocean 122

Kirinyaga *Peak* Kenya *var.* Mount Kenya 49 D5

Kiritimati *Island* Kiribati *var.* Christmas Island 127 G2

Kirkenes Norway 64 E2

Kirklareli Turkey 96 A2

Kirkpatrick, Mount *Peak* Antarctica 132 D4

Kirksville Missouri, USA 23 G4

Kirkūk Iraq 100 B3

Kirkwall Scotland, UK 68 C2

Kirman *see* Kermān

Kirov Russian Federation 90 C4 94 B3

Kirovabad *see* Gäncä

Kirovakan *see* Vanadzor

Kirovohrad Ukraine 89 E8

Kiruna Sweden 64 C3

Kisangani Zaire *prev.* Stanleyville 57 D5

Kishinev *see* Chişinău

Kiska Island *Island* Alaska, USA 16 A2

Kismaayo Somalia 55 D6

Kisumu Kenya 55 C6

Kitakyūshū Japan 111 A5

Kitami Japan 110 D2

Kitchener Canada 18 C5

Kitwe Zambia 58 D2

Kivu, Lake *Lake* Rwanda/Zaire 55 B6 57 E6

Kızıl Irmak *River* Turkey 96 C2

Kizil Kum *see* Kyzyl Kum

Kizyl-Arvat *see* Gyzylarbat

Kjølen Mountains *Mountain range* Sweden *see* Kölen 60 D2

Kladno Czech Republic 79 A5

Klagenfurt Austria 75 D7

Klaipėda Lithuania *Ger.* Memel 86 B4

Klamath Falls Oregon, USA 24 B4

Ključ Bosnia & Herzegovina 80 B3

Knin Croatia 80 B4

Knittelfeld Austria 75 D7

Knoxville Tennessee, USA 29 E1

Knud Rasmussen Land *Region* Greenland 62 B2

Kōbe Japan 111 C5

Koblenz Germany 75 A5

Kobryn Belarus 87 B6

Kocaeli *see* İzmit

Kočani Macedonia 81 E5

Kōchi Japan 111 B6

Kodiak Alaska, USA 16 C3

Kodiak Island *Island* Alaska, USA 16 C3

Kohīma India 115 H3

Kohtla-Järve Estonia 86 D2

Kokand Uzbekistan *var.* Khokand, *Uzb.* Qŭqon 103 E2

Kokchetav Kazakhstan 94 C4

Kokkola Finland 64 D4

Koko Nor *see* Qinghai Hu

Kokshaal-Tau *Mountain range* Kyrgyzstan 103 G2

Kola Peninsula *see* Kol'skiy Poluostrov

Kolda Senegal 52 B3

Kölen *see* Kjølen Mountains

Kolguyev, Ostrov *Island* Russian Federation 90 D2

Kolhumadulu Atoll *Island* Maldives 116 C5

Kolka Latvia 86 B2

Köln Germany *Eng.* Cologne 75 A5

Kol'skiy Poluostrov *Peninsula* Russian Federation *Eng.* Kola Peninsula 61 F1 90 C2

Kolwezi Zaire 57 D7

Kolyma Range *Mountain range* Russian Federation 93 G2

Komárno Slovakia *Ger.* Komorn, *Hung.* Komárom 79 C6

Komárom *see* Komárno

Kommunizma, Pik *see* Communism Peak

Komoé *River* Ivory Coast 53 E4

Komorn *see* Komárno

Komotau *see* Chomutov

Komotiní Greece 84 D3

Komsomol'sk Turkmenistan 102 D3

Komsomol'sk-na-Amure Russian Federation 95 G4

Kondoz *see* Kunduz

Kondūz *see* Kunduz

Köneürgench *see* Këneurgench

Kong Christian IX Land *Region* Greenland 62 D3

Kong Christian X Land *Region* Greenland 62 D3

Kong Frederik VI Kyst *Region* Greenland 62 C4

Kong Frederik VIII Land *Region* Greenland 62 D3

Kong Frederik IX Land *Region* Greenland 62 C4

Kongsvinger Norway 65 B6

Konia *see* Konya

Königgrätz *see* Hradec Králové

Königsberg *see* Kaliningrad

Konispol Albania 81 D7

Konjic Bosnia & Herzegovina 80 C4

Konya Turkey *prev.* Konia 96 C4

Kopaonik *Mountains* Yugoslavia 81 D4

Koper Slovenia 80 A3

Koprivnica Croatia 80 B2

Korçë Albania 81 D6

Korčula *Island* Croatia 80 B4

Korea Strait *Sea feature* Japan/South Korea 108–109 E5

Korhogo Ivory Coast 52 D4

Korinthiakós Kólpos *Sea feature* Greece *Eng.* Gulf of Corinth 85 B5

Kórinthos Greece *Eng.* Corinth 85 B5

Kōriyama Japan 111 D4

Korla China 106 B3

Koror *Capital of* Palau 126 A1

Körös *River* Hungary 79 D7

Korosten' Ukraine 88 D1

Kortrijk Belgium 67 A6

Kos *Island* Greece 85 E6

Kosciusko, Mount *Peak* Australia 124 C4

Košice Slovakia *Ger.* Kaschau, *Hung.* Kassa 79 D6

Köslin *see* Koszalin

Kosovo *Province* Yugoslavia 81 D5

Kosovska Mitrovica Yugoslavia 80 D4

Kosrae *Island* Micronesia 126 C2

Koszalin Poland *Ger.* Köslin 78 B2

Kota India 114 D4

Kota Bharu Malaysia 120 B3

Kota Kinabalu Malaysia 120 D3

Kotka Finland 65 E5

Kotlas NW Russia 90 C4

Kotto *River* C Africa 56 D4

Koudougou Burkina 53 E4

Kourou French Guiana 39 H2

Kousséri Cameroon 56 B3

Kouvola Finland 65 E5

Kovel' Ukraine 88 C1

Kovno *see* Kaunas

Kowno *see* Kaunas

Kozáni Greece 84 B4

Kozhikode *see* Calicut

Kra, Isthmus of *Coastal feature*
Myanmar/Thailand 119 B6

Kragujevac Yugoslavia 80 D4

Krakatau *Peak* Indonesia 104 D5

Krakau *see* Kraków

Kraków Poland *Eng.* Cracow,
Ger. Krakau 79 D5

Kraljevo Yugoslavia 80 D4

Kranj Slovenia 80 A2

Krasnodar Russian Federation
91 A6

Krasnovodsk *see* Turkmenbashy

Krasnoyarsk Russian Federation
94 D4

Krasnyy Luch Ukraine 89 G5

Kremenchuk Ukraine 89 F2

Kremenchuts'ke
Vodoskhovyshche *Reservoir*
Ukraine 89 E2

Krems an der Donau Austria
75 E6

Kretinga Lithuania
Ger. Krottingen 86 B3

Kribi Cameroon 57 B5

Krichev *see* Krychaw

Krishna *River* India 116 C1

Kristiansand Norway 65 A6

Kristianstad Sweden 65 B7

Kríti *Island* Greece *Eng.* Crete
85 C7

Kritikó Pélagos *see* Crete, Sea of

Krivoy Rog *see* Kryvyy Rih

Krk *Island* Croatia 80 A3

Kroonstad South Africa 58 D4

Krottingen *see* Kretinga

Krung Thep *see* Bangkok

Kruševac Yugoslavia 81 D4

Krychaw Belarus
Rus. Krichev 87 E6

Krym *see* Crimea

Kryvyy Rih Ukraine
Rus. Krivoy Rog 89 E3

Kuala Lumpur *Capital of*
Malaysia 120 B3

Kuala Terengganu Malaysia
120 B3

Kuantan Malaysia 120 B3

Kuba *see* Quba

Kuching Malaysia 120 C3

Kuçovë Albania *prev.* Qyteti
Stalin 81 D6

Kuito Angola 58 C2

Kuldīga Latvia *Ger.* Goldingen
86 B3

Kullorsuaq Greenland 62 B3

Kulyab SW Tajikistan 103 E3

Kum *see* Qom

Kuma *River* Russian Federation
91 B7

Kumamoto Japan 111 A6

Kumanovo Macedonia 81 E5

Kumasi Ghana 53 E5

Kumayri *see* Gyumri 97 F2

Kumbo Cameroon 56 B4

Kumon Range *Mountain range*
Myanmar 118 B1

Kunashir *Island* Japan/Russian
Federation (disputed) 110 E1

Kunduz Afghanistan
var. Kondūz, Qondūz, Kondoz
103 E3

Kunja-Urgenč *see* Këneurgench

Kunlun Mountains *see* Kunlun
Shan

Kunlun Shan *Mountain range*
China *Eng.* Kunlun Mountains
104 C2 106 B3

Kunming China 109 A6

Kununurra Australia 128 D3

Kupang Indonesia 120 E5

Kür *see* Kura

Kura *River* Azerbaijan/Georgia
Az. Kür 96 G2

Kurashiki Japan 111 B5

Küre Dağları *Mountains* Turkey
96 C2

Kuressaare Estonia
prev. Kingissepp,
Ger. Arensburg 86 C2

Kurgan-Tyube Tajikistan 103 E3

Kurile Islands *Islands* Pacific
Ocean 105 F1

Kurile Trench *Undersea feature*
Pacific Ocean 122 C2

Kurmuk Sudan 54 C4

Kurnool India 116 D2

Kuršėnai Lithuania 86 B4

Kushiro Japan 110 E2

Kushka *see* Gushgy

Kustanay Kazakhstan 94 C4

Kütahya Turkey *prev.* Kutaiah
96 B3

Kutaiah *see* Kütahya

K'ut'aisi Georgia 97 F2

Kutch, Rann of *see* Kachch,
Rann of

Kuujjuaq Canada 19 E2

Kuujjuarapik Canada 18 D2

Kuusamo Finland 64 E3

Kuwait *Country* SW Asia 100 C4

Kuwait City *Capital of* Kuwait
100 C4

Kuytun China 106 B3

Kwangju South Korea 109 E5

Kwango *River* Zaire 57 C7

Kykládes *Island group* Greece
prev. Kikládhes, *Eng.* Cyclades
85 D6

Kyrenia *see* Girne

Kyrgyzstan *Country* C Asia
var. Kirghizia 103

Kýthira *Island* Greece 85 B6

Kyushu-Palau Ridge *Undersea
feature* Pacific Ocean 111 B7
121 G1

Kyyiv *see* Kiev

Kyzyl Kum *Desert*
Kazakhstan/Uzbekistan
var. Kizil Kum, *Uzb.* Qizilqum
92 C3

Kyōto Japan 111 C5

Kyūshū *Island* Japan 111 B6

Kzyl-Orda Kazakhstan 94 B5

L

Laâyoune Western Sahara 50 B3

Labé Guinea 52 C4

Laborca *see* Laborec

Laborec *River* Slovakia
Hung. Laborca 79 E5

Labrador *Region* Canada
19 F2

Labrador Basin *Undersea feature*
Atlantic Ocean 15 G2 19 G1

Labrador City Canada 19 E3

Labrador Sea Atlantic Ocean
62 B5

Laccadive Islands see
  Lakshadweep
La Ceiba Honduras 32 D2
La Coruña see A Coruña
La Crosse Wisconsin, USA
  20 A2
Ladoga, Lake see Ladozhskoye
  Ozero
Ladozhskoye Ozero Lake
  Russian Federation Eng. Lake
  Ladoga 90 B3
Lae Papua New Guinea 126 B3
La Esperanza Honduras 32 C2
Lafayette Louisiana, USA 28 B3
Lågen River Norway 65 B5
Laghouat Algeria 50 D2
Lagos Nigeria 53 F5
Lagos Portugal 72 C4
La Grande Oregon, USA 24 C3
La Habana see Havana
Lahore Pakistan 114 C2
Laï Chad 56 C4
Laila see Laylá
Lajes Brazil 42 D3
Lake District Region England,
  UK 69 C5
Lakewood Colorado, USA
  22 D4
Lakshadweep Island group India
  Eng. Laccadive Islands 116 B2
La Ligua Chile 44 B4
La Louvière Belgium 67 B6
Lambaré Paraguay 42 B3
Lambaréné Gabon 57 B6
Lambert Glacier Ice feature
  Antarctica 133 G2
Lamía Greece 85 B5
Lampedusa Island Italy 77 B8
Lampione Island Italy 77 B8
Lancaster England, UK 69 D5
Lancaster California, USA 25 C7
Lancaster Sound Sea feature
  Canada 17 G2
Landsberg see Gorzów
  Wielkopolski
Land's End Coastal feature
  England, UK 69 B7
Lang Son Vietnam 118 D3
Länkäran Azerbaijan
  Rus. Lenkoran' 97 H3
Lansing Michigan, USA 20 C3
Lanzarote Island Spain 50 B3
Lanzhou China 108 B4

Laon France 70 D3
La Oroya Peru 40 B3
Laos Country SE Asia 118
La Palma Island Spain 50 A3
La Paz Capital of Bolivia 40 C4
La Paz Mexico 30 B3
La Pérouse Strait Sea feature
  Japan 110 D1
Lapland Region N Europe 64 C3
La Plata Argentina 44 D4
Lappeenranta Finland 65 E5
Laptev Sea see Laptevykh, More
Laptevykh, More Arctic Ocean
  Eng. Laptev Sea 12 E3 95 F2
L'Aquila Italy 76 C4
Laramie Wyoming, USA 22 C4
Laredo Texas, USA 27 F5
La Rioja Argentina 44 C3
Lárisa Greece 84 B4
Lārkāna Pakistan 114 B3
Larnaca Cyprus var. Larnaka,
  Larnax 96 C5
Larnaka see Larnaca
Larnax see Larnaca
La Rochelle France 70 B4
La Roche-sur-Yon France 70 B4
La Romana Dominican Republic
  34 E3
Las Cruces New Mexico, USA
  26 D3
La Serena Chile 44 B3
La Spezia Italy 76 B3
Las Piedras Uruguay 42 C5
Las Tablas Panama 33 F5
Las Vegas Nevada, USA 25 D7
Latakia see Al Lādhiqīyah
Latvia Country NE Europe 86
Launceston Tasmania 130 B3
Laurentian Basin see Canada
  Basin
Laurentian Plateau Upland
  Canada 15 F3
Lausanne Switzerland 75 A7
Laval France 70 B3
Lawton Oklahoma, USA 27 F2
Laylá Saudi Arabia 101 C5
Lebanon Country SW Asia
  98-99
Lebu Chile 45 B5
Lecce Italy 77 E5
Leduc Canada 17 E5
Leeds England, UK 69 D5

Leeuwarden Netherlands
  66 D1
Leeuwin, Cape Coastal feature
  Australia 129 B6
Leeward Islands Island group
  West Indies 35 G3
Lefkáda Island Greece
  prev. Levkás 85 A5
Lefkoşa see Nicosia
Lefkosia see Nicosia
Legaspi Philippines 120 E2
Legnica Poland Ger. Liegnitz
  78 B4
Le Havre France 70 B3
Leicester England, UK 69 D6
Leiden Netherlands 66 C3
Leipzig Germany 74 C4
Leivádia Greece 85 B5
Leizhou Bandao Peninsula
  China 109 C7
Lek River Netherlands 66 C4
Le Léman see Geneva, Lake
Lelystad Netherlands 66 D3
Léman, Lac see Geneva, Lake
Le Mans France 70 B3
Lemesos see Limassol
Lemnos see Límnos
Lena River Russian Federation
  95 F3
Leninabad see Khudzhand
Leninakan see Gyumri
Leningrad see St Petersburg
Leninsk see Chardzhev
Lenkoran' see Länkäran
León Mexico 31 N7
León Nicaragua 32 C3
León Spain 72 D2
Léopoldville see Kinshasa
Lepel' see Lyepyel'
Le Puy France 71 C5
Lérida see Lleida
Lerwick Scotland, UK 68 D1
Lesbos see Lésvos
Leskovac Yugoslavia 80 E4
Lesotho Country southern
  Africa 58
Lesser Antarctica Region
  Antarctica 134 C2
Lesser Antilles Island group
  West Indies 35 G4
Lésvos Island Greece
  Eng. Lesbos 83 F3 85 D4

Lethbridge Canada 17 F5
Leti, Kepulauan *Island group* Indonesia 121 F5
Leuven Belgium 67 C6
Leverkusen Germany 75 A5
Levkás *see* Lefkáda
Lewis *Island* Scotland, UK 68 B2
Lewiston Idaho, USA 24 C2
Lewiston Maine, USA 21 G2
Lexington Kentucky, USA 20 C5
Leyte *Island* Philippines 121 E2
Lezhë Albania 81 D5
Lhasa China 106 C5
Liangyungang China 109 D5
Liaoyuan China 108 D3
Libau *see* Liepāja
Liberec Czech Republic *Ger.* Reichenberg 78 B4
Liberia *Country* W Africa 52
Liberia Costa Rica 32 D4
Libreville *Capital of* Gabon 57 A5
Libya *Country* N Africa 51
Libyan Desert *Desert* N Africa 48 C3
Liechtenstein *Country* C Europe 75 B7
Liège Belgium 67 D6
Liegnitz *see* Legnica
Lienz Austria 75 D7
Liepāja Latvia *Ger.* Libau 86 B3
Liffey *River* Ireland 69 B5
Ligurian Sea Mediterranean Sea 71 E6
Likasi Zaire 57 E8
Lille France 70 C4
Lillehammer Norway 65 B5
Lilongwe *Capital of* Malawi 59 E2
Lima *Capital of* Peru 40 B4
Lima Ohio, USA 20 C4
Limassol Cyprus *var.* Lemesos 96 C5
Limerick Ireland 69 A6
Límnos *Island* Greece *var.* Lemnos 84 C4
Limoges France 70 C5
Limón Costa Rica 33 E4
Limpopo *River* southern Africa 58 D3
Linares Chile 44 B4
Linares Spain 73 E4

Lincoln England, UK 69 D5
Lincoln Nebraska, USA 23 F4
Lincoln Sea Arctic Ocean 62 B1
Linden Guyana 39 G2
Lindi *River* Zaire 55 C8
Line Islands *Island group* Kiribati 127 H3
Lingga, Kepulauan *Island group* Indonesia 120 B4
Linköping Sweden 65 C6
Linosa *Island* Italy 77 C8
Linz Austria 75 D6
Lion, Golfe du *Sea feature* Mediterranean Sea 82 C2
Lipari *Island* Italy 77 D6
Lipari Islands *see* Isole Eolie
Lira Uganda 55 B6
Lisbon *Capital of* Portugal *Port.* Lisboa 72 B4
Litang China 109 A5
Litani *River* SW Asia 89 B4
Lithuania *Country* E Europe 86-87
Little Andaman *Island* India 117 G2
Little Minch *Sea feature* Scotland, UK 68 B3
Little Rock Arkansas, USA 28 B2
Liuzhou China 109 B6
Liverpool England, UK 69 D5
Livingston, Lake *Lake* Texas, USA 27 H3
Livingstone Zambia 58 D3
Livno Bosnia & Herzegovina 80 B4
Livorno Italy 76 B3
Ljubljana *Capital of* Slovenia 80 A2
Ljusnan *River* Sweden 65 B5
Llanos *Region* Colombia/Venezuela 39 D2
Lleida Spain *Cast.* Lérida 73 F2
Lobatse Botswana 58 D4
Lobito Angola 58 B2
Locarno Switzerland 75 B8
Lodja Zaire 57 D6
Łódź Poland *Rus.* Lodz 78 D4
Lofoten *Island group* Norway 64 B3
Logan, Mount *Peak* Canada 14 C2

Logroño Spain 73 E2
Loire *River* France 70 B4
Loja Ecuador 38 A5
Lokitaung Kenya 55 C5
Loksa Estonia *Ger.* Loxa 86 D2
Lombok *Island* Indonesia 120 D5
Lomé *Capital of* Togo 53 F5
Lomond, Loch *Lake* Scotland, UK 68 C4
Lomonosov Ridge *Undersea feature* Arctic Ocean *var.* Harris Ridge 12 D4
London Canada 18 C5
London *Capital of* UK 69 E6
Londonderry Northern Ireland, UK 69 B5
Londonderry, Cape *Coastal feature* Australia 124 B2 128 C2
Londrina Brazil 42 D2
Long Beach California, USA 25 C8
Long Island *Island* Bahamas 34 D2
Long Island *Island* NE USA 21 G3
Longreach Australia 126 B5
Longview Texas, USA 27 G3
Longview Washington, USA 24 B2
Longyearbyen Svalbard 63 G2
Lop Nur *Lake* China 106 C3
Lorca Spain 73 F4
Lord Howe Rise *Undersea feature* Pacific Ocean 122 C4
Lorient France 70 A3
Los Alamos New Mexico, USA 26 D2
Los Angeles California, USA 25 C8
Loslau *see* Wodzisław Śląski
Los Mochis Mexico 30 C3
Losonc *see* Lučenec
Losontz *see* Lučenec
Lot *River* France 71 B5
Louangphrabang Laos 118 C3
Loubomo Congo 57 B6
Louisiana *State* USA 28 B3
Louisville Kentucky, USA 20 C5
Lovech Bulgaria 84 C2
Lower California *see* Baja California

Loxa *see* Loksa
Loyauté, Îles *Island group* New Caledonia 126 D5
Loznica Yugoslavia 80 C3
Luanda *Capital of* Angola 58 B1
Luanshya Zambia 58 D2
Lubānas Ezers *Lake* Latvia 86 D4
Lubango Angola 58 B2
Lubbock Texas, USA 27 E2
Lübeck Germany 74 C3
Lublin Poland *Rus.* Lyublin 78 E4
Lubny Ukraine 89 F2
Lubumbashi Zaire 57 E8
Lucapa Angola 58 C1
Lucena Philippines 120 E1
Lučenec Slovakia *Hung.* Losonc, *Ger.* Losontz 79 D6
Lucerne *see* Luzern
Lucknow India 115 E3
Lüderitz Namibia 58 B4
Ludhiāna India 114 D2
Lugano Switzerland 75 B8
Lugo Spain 72 C1
Luhans'k Ukraine 89 H3
Luleå Sweden 64 D4
Lumsden New Zealand 131 F5
Luninyets Belarus 97 C6
Lusaka *Capital of* Zambia 58 D2
Lushnjë Albania 81 D6
Lüt, Baḥrat *see* Dead Sea
Luts'k Ukraine 88 C1
Lutzow-Holm Bay *Sea feature* Antarctica 133 F1
Luxembourg *Country* W Europe 67 D8
Luxembourg *Capital of* Luxembourg 67 D8
Luxor Egypt 54 B2
Luzern Switzerland *Fr.* Lucerne 75 B7
Luzon *Island* Philippines 121 E1
Luzon Strait *Sea feature* Philippines/Taiwan 105 E3
L'viv Ukraine *Rus.* L'vov 88 B2
L'vov *see* L'viv
Lyepyel' Belarus *Rus.* Lepel' 87 D5
Lyon France 71 D5
Lyublin *see* Lublin

M

Ma'ān Jordan 99 B6
Maas *River* W Europe *var.* Meuse 66 D4
Maastricht Netherlands 67 D6
Macao *External territory* Portugal, E Asia *var.* Macau 109 C7
Macapá Brazil 41 F1
Macau *see* Macao
Macdonald Islands *Islands* Indian Ocean 113 B7
Macdonnell Ranges *Mountains* Australia 128 D4
Macedonia *Country* SE Europe officially Former Yugoslav Republic of Macedonia, *abbrev.* FYR Macedonia 81
Maceió Brazil 41 H3
Machakos Kenya 55 C6
Machala Ecuador 38 A5
Mackay Australia 126 B5 130 C1
Mackay, Lake *Lake* Australia 128 D4
Mackenzie *River* Canada 17 E4
Mackenzie Bay *Sea feature* Atlantic Ocean 133 G2
Mâcon France 70 D5
Macon Georgia, USA 29 E2
Madagascar *Country* Indian Ocean 59
Madagascar Basin *Undersea feature* Indian Ocean 113 B5
Madagascar Ridge *Undersea feature* Indian Ocean 113 A5
Madang Papua New Guinea 126 B3
Madeira *River* Bolivia/Brazil 40 D2
Madeira *Island group* Portugal 50 A2
Madhya Pradesh *State* India 115 E4
Madison Wisconsin, USA 20 B3
Madona Latvia *Ger.* Modohn 86 D3
Madras India 117 E2
Madre de Dios *River* Bolivia/Peru 40 C3
Madrid *Capital of* Spain 73 E3
Madurai India 116 D3

Magadan Russian Federation 95 G3
Magallanes *see* Punta Arenas
Magallanes, Estrecho de *see* Magellan, Strait of
Magdalena *River* Colombia 38 B2
Magdeburg Germany 74 C4
Magellan, Strait of *Sea feature* S South America *Sp.* Estrecho de Magallanes 37 B7
Maggiore, Lake *Lake* Italy/Switzerland 75 B8
Mahajanga Madagascar 59 G2
Mahalapye Botswana 58 D3
Mahanādi India 115 F5
Mahārāshtra *State* India 114 D5
Mahé *Island* Seychelles 59 H1
Mahilyow Belarus *Rus.* Mogilëv 87 E6
Mährisch-Ostrau *see* Ostrava
Maicao Colombia 38 C1
Maiduguri Nigeria 53 H4
Maimana *see* Meymaneh
Maine *State* USA 21 G1
Mainz Germany 75 B5
Maiquetía Venezuela 38 D1
Maíz, Islas del *Islands* Nicaragua 33 E3 34 B5
Majorca *see* Mallorca
Majuro *Island* Marshall Islands 126 D1
Makarska Croatia 80 B4
Makeni Sierra Leone 52 C4
Makeyevka *see* Makiyivka
Makgadikgadi *Salt pan* Botswana 58 D3
Makhachkala Russian Federation 91 B7 94 A4
Makiyivka Ukraine *Rus.* Makeyevka 89 G5
Makkah Saudi Arabia *Eng.* Mecca 101 A5
Makkovik Canada 19 G2
Makurdi Nigeria 53 G4
Malabo *Capital of* Equatorial Guinea 57 A5
Malacca *see* Melaka
Malacca, Strait of *Sea feature* Indonesia/ Malaysia 104 C4 119 C8

Maladzyechna Belarus
Rus. Molodechno,
Pol. Molodeczno 87 C5

Málaga Spain 72 D5

Malakal Sudan 55 B5

Malang Indonesia 120 D5

Malanje Angola 58 B2

Malatya Turkey 97 E3

Malawi *Country* southern
Africa 59

Malay Peninsula *Peninsula*
Malaysia/Thailand 119 D8

Malaysia *Country* Asia 120

Maldive Ridge *Undersea feature*
Indian Ocean 112 C4

Maldives *Country* Indian Ocean
116

Male' *Capital of* Maldives
116 C4

Mali *Country* W Africa 53

Malindi Kenya 55 C7

Mallorca *Island* Spain
Eng. Majorca 73 H3

Malmö Sweden 65 B5

Malta *Country* Mediterranean
Sea 77 C8

Malta Montana, USA 22 C1

Malta Channel *Sea feature*
Mediterranean Sea 77 C7

Maluku *Island group* Indonesia
var. Moluccas 105 E4 121 F4

Maluku, Laut Pacific Ocean
Eng. Molucca Sea 121 F4

Māmallapuram India 117 E2

Mamberamo *River* Indonesia
121 H4

Mamoudzou *Capital of* Mayotte
59 G2

Man Ivory Coast 52 D4

Man, Isle of *Island* UK 69 C5

Manado Indonesia 120 F3

Managua *Capital of* Nicaragua
32 D3

Manama *Capital of* Bahrain
Ar. Al Manāmah 101 C5

Mananjary Madagascar 59 G3

Manaus Brazil 40 D2

Manchester England, UK 69 D5

Manchester New Hampshire,
USA 21 G2

Manchuria *Region* China 108 D3

Manchurian Plain *Plain* E Asia
105 E1

Mandalay Myanmar 118 B3

Mangalia Romania 88 D5

Mangalore India 116 C2

Manguéni, Plateau du *Upland*
Niger 53 H2

Manicouagan, Réservoir
Reservoir Canada 19 E3

Manila *Capital of* Philippines
120 E1

Manisa Turkey *prev.* Saruhan
96 A3

Manitoba *Province* Canada
17 G4

Manizales Colombia 38 B3

Manjimup Australia 129 B6

Manlitsoq Greenland 62 B4

Mannar Sri Lanka 117 E3

Mannar, Gulf of *Sea feature*
Indian Ocean 116 D3

Mannheim Germany 75 B5

Mannu *River* Italy 77 A5

Manono Zaire 57 E7

Mansel Island *Island* Canada
18 C1

Manta Ecuador 38 A4

Mantes-la-Jolie France 70 C3

Mantova Italy *Eng.* Mantua
76 B2

Mantua *see* Mantova

Manzhouli China 107 F1

Mao Chad 56 B3

Maoke, Pegunungan *Mountains*
Indonesia 121 H4

Maputo *Capital of* Mozambique
59 E4

Mar, Serra do *Mountains* Brazil
36 D4

Maracaibo Venezuela 38 C1

Maracaibo, Lago de *Inlet*
Venezuela 38 C1

Maracay Venezuela 38 D1

Maradi Niger 53 G3

Marajó, Ilha de *Island* Brazil
41 F2

Marañón *River* Peru 40 B2

Maraş *see* Kahramanmaraş

Marash *see* Kahramanmaraş

Marbella Spain 72 D5

Mar Chiquita, Laguna *Salt lake*
Argentina 44 D3

Mardān Pakistan 114 C1

Mar del Plata Argentina 45 D5

Mardin Turkey 97 E4

Margarita, Isla de *Island*
Venezuela 35 F3 39 E1

Märgow, Dasht-e- *Desert*
Afghanistan 102 C5

Mariana Trench *Undersea feature*
Pacific Ocean 122 C2

Marías, Islas *Islands* Mexico
30 C4

Maribor Slovenia 80 B2

Marie Byrd Land *Region*
Antarctica 132 C3

Mariehamn Finland 65 D6

Marijampolė Lithuania
prev. Kapsukas 86 B4

Marília Brazil 41 F5 42 D2

Maringá Brazil 42 D2

Marion, Lake *Lake* South
Carolina, USA 29 F2

Mariscal Estigarribia Paraguay
42 B2

Maritsa *River* SE Europe 84 D3

Mariupol' Ukraine
prev. Shdanov 89 G4

Marka Somalia 55 D6

Markham, Mount *Peak*
Antarctica 132 B4

Marmara, Sea of *see* Marmara
Denizi

Marmara Denizi Turkey
Eng. Sea of Marmara 96 B2

Marne *River* France 70 D3

Maroua Cameroon 56 B3

Marowijne *River* French
Guiana/Suriname 39 H3

Marqueses Islands *Island group*
French Polynesia *Fr.* Îles
Marquises 125 H2

Marquette Michigan, USA 20 B1

Marquisas, Îles *see* Marquesas
Islands

Marrakech Morocco
Eng. Marrakesh 50 B2

Marsala Italy 77 C7

Marseille France 71 D6

Marshall Islands *Country* Pacific
Ocean 126-127

Marsh Island *Island* Louisiana,
USA 29 B4

Martin Slovakia *prev.* Turčiansky
Svätý Martin,
Ger. Sankt Martin,
Hung. Turócszentmárton
79 C5

Martinique *External territory*
France, West Indies 35

Mary Turkmenistan *prev.* Merv 102 C3

Maryland *State* USA 21 F4

Mascarene Islands *Island group* Indian Ocean 59 H3

Mascarene Plateau *Undersea feature* Indian Ocean 113 B5

Maseru *Capital of* Lesotho 58 D4

Mashhad Iran *var.* Meshed 100 E3

Masindi Uganda 55 B6

Mason City Iowa, USA 23 F3

Masqaṭ *see* Muscat

Massachusetts *State* USA 21 G3

Massawa Eritrea 54 C4

Massif Central *Upland* France 71 C5

Massoukou Gabon 57 B6

Masterton New Zealand 131 G3

Matadi Zaire 57 B7

Matagalpa Nicaragua 32 D3

Matamoros Mexico 31 E2

Matanzas Cuba 34 B2

Matara Sri Lanka 117 E4

Mataró Spain 73 G2

Mato Grosso, Planalto de *Upland* Brazil 41 E3

Matosinhos Portugal 72 C2

Matrûh Egypt 54 B1

Matsue Japan 111 B5

Matsuyama Japan 111 B5

Maturín Venezuela 39 E1

Maun Botswana 58 D3

Mauritania *Country* W Africa 52

Mauritius *Country* Indian Ocean 59 H3

Mayaguana *Island* Bahamas 34 D2

Mayotte *External territory* France, Indian Ocean 59 G2

Mayyit, Al Baḥr al *see* Dead Sea

Mazâr-e Sharîf Afghanistan 102 D3

Mazatenango Guatemala 32 B2

Mazatlán Mexico 30 C3

Mažeikiai Lithuania 86 B3

Mazury *Region* Poland 78 D3

Mazyr Belarus *Rus.* Mozyr' 87 D7

Mbabane *Capital of* Swaziland 59 E4

Mbala Zambia 59 E1

Mbale Uganda 55 C6

Mbandaka Zaire 57 C5

Mbeya Tanzania 55 B8

Mbuji-Mayi Zaire 57 D7

McKinley, Mount *see* Denali

McMurdo Sound *Sea feature* Antarctica 133 B5

Mead, Lake *Lake* SW USA 25 D7 26 A1

Mecca *see* Makkah

Mechelen Belgium 67 C5

Medan Indonesia 120 A3

Medellín Colombia 38 B2

Médenine Tunisia 51 F2

Medford Oregon, USA 24 B4

Medina *see* Al Madînah

Mediterranean Sea *Atlantic Ocean* 82-83

Meekatharra Australia 129 B5

Meerut India 114 D3

Mek'elê Ethiopia 54 C4

Meknès Morocco 50 C2

Mekong *River* SE Asia 104 D3

Mekong Delta *Wetlands* Vietnam 119 E6

Melaka Malaysia *prev.* Malacca 120 B3

Melanesia *Region* Pacific Ocean 124-125 126-127

Melbourne Australia 130 B4

Melbourne Florida, USA 29 F4

Melilla *External territory* Spain, N Africa 50 C1

Melitopol' Ukraine 89 F4

Melo Uruguay 42 D4

Melville Island *Island* Australia 128 D2

Melville Island *Island* Canada 17 E2

Memel *see* Klaipėda

Memel *see* Neman

Memphis Tennessee, USA 28 C2

Mende France 71 C6

Mendi Papua New Guinea 126 B3

Mendoza Argentina 44 B4

Menongue Angola 58 C2

Menorca *Island* Spain *Eng.* Minorca 73 H3

Mentawai, Kepulauan *Island group* Indonesia 120 A4

Meppel Netherlands 66 D2

Merced California, USA 25 B6

Mercedario *Peak* Argentina 37 B5

Mercedes Argentina 44 C4

Mercedes Uruguay 42 B5

Mergui Myanmar 119 B5

Mergui Archipelago *Island chain* Myanmar 119 B6

Mérida Mexico 31 H3

Mérida Spain 72 D4

Mérida Venezuela 38 C2

Meridian Mississippi, USA 28 C3

Merredin Australia 129 B6

Mersin Turkey *var.* İçel 96 C4

Meru Kenya 55 C5

Merv *see* Mary

Mesa Arizona, USA 26 B2

Meshed *see* Mashhad

Messina Italy 77 D6

Messina, Stretto di *Sea feature* Ionian Sea / Tyrrhenian Sea 77 D7

Mesters Vig Greenland 62 D3

Mestre Italy 76 C2

Meta *River* Colombia / Venezuela 38 C2

Metković Croatia 80 C4

Metz France 70 D3

Meuse *River* W Europe *var.* Maas 70 D3

Mexicali Mexico 30 A1

Mexicana, Altiplanicie *see* Mexico, Plateau of

Mexico *Country* North America 30-31

México, Golfo de *see* Mexico, Gulf of

Mexico, Gulf of *Sea feature* Atlantic Ocean / Caribbean Sea 46 A4

Mexico, Plateau of *Upland* Mexico *Sp.* Altiplanicie Mexicana 14 D4

Mexico City *Capital of* Mexico *Sp.* Ciudad de México 31 E4

Meymaneh Afghanistan *var.* Maimana 102 D4

Mezen' *River* Russian Federation 90 D3

Miami Florida, USA 29 F5

Michigan *State* USA 20 C2

Michigan, Lake *Lake* USA 20 C2

Micronesia *Country* Pacific Ocean 126

Micronesia *Region* Pacific Ocean 126-127

Mid Atlantic Ridge *Undersea feature* Atlantic Ocean 46 B4

Middelburg South Africa 58 D5

Middle America Trench *Undersea feature* Pacific Ocean 36 A1

Middle Andaman *Island* India 117 G2

Middlesbrough England, UK 69 D5

Mid-Indian Ridge *Undersea feature* Indian Ocean 113 C5

Midland Texas, USA 27 E2

Mikhaylovka Russian Federation 91 B6

Mikkeli Finland 65 E5

Míkonos *Island* Greece 85 D6

Milagro Ecuador 38 A4

Milan *see* Milano

Milano Italy *Eng.* Milan 76 B2

Mildura Australia 130 B3

Miles Australia 130 C2

Miles City Montana, USA 22 C2

Milford Haven Wales, UK 69 C6

Milford Sound New Zealand 131 E4

Mílos *Island* Greece 85 C6

Milparinka Australia 130 B2

Milwaukee Wisconsin, USA 20 B3

Minatitlán Mexico 31 G4

Mindanao *Island* Philippines 121 F2

Mindoro *Island* Philippines 121 E2

Mindoro Strait *Sea feature* South China Sea/Sulu Sea 121 E2

Mingáçevir Azerbaijan *Rus.* Mingechaur 97 G2

Mingechaur *see* Mingáçevir

Minho *River* Portugal/Spain *Sp.* Miño 72 C2

Minicoy Island *Island* India 116 C3

Minneapolis Minnesota, USA 23 F2

Minnesota *State* USA 23 F1

Miño *River* Portugal/Spain *Port.* Minho 72 C1

Minorca *see* Menorca

Minot North Dakota, USA 22 D1

Minto, Lake *Lake* Canada 18 D2

Minsk *Capital of* Belarus 87 C5

Miranda de Ebro Spain 73 E2

Mirim, Lake *Lagoon* Brazil/Uruguay *var.* Mirim Lagoon 42 C5

Mirtóo Pelagos *Sea feature* Mediterranean Sea 85 C6

Miskitos Cayos *Islands* Nicaragua 33 E2

Miskolc Hungary 79 D6

Mişrātah Libya 51 F2

Mississippi *State* USA 28 C2

Mississippi *River* USA 15 E4

Mississippi Delta *Wetlands* USA 15 E4

Missoula Montana, USA 22 B2

Missouri *State* USA 23 G5

Missouri *River* USA 23 G4

Mistassini, Lake *Lake* Canada 18 D3

Mitau *see* Jelgava

Mitchell South Dakota, USA 23 E3

Mitilíni Greece 84 D4

Mito Japan 110 D4

Miyazaki Japan 111 B6

Mjøsa *Lake* Norway 65 B5

Mljet *Island* Croatia 81 C5

Mmabatho South Africa 58 D4

Mo Norway 64 C3

Mobile Alabama, USA 28 C3

Moçambique Mozambique 59 F2

Mocímboa da Praia Mozambique 59 F2

Mocoa Colombia 38 B4

Mocuba Mozambique 59 F2

Modena Italy 76 B3

Modesto California, USA 25 B6

Mödling Austria 75 E6

Modohn *see* Madona

Modriča Bosnia & Herzegovina 80 C3

Mogadiscio *see* Mogadishu

Mogadishu *Capital of* Somalia *Som.* Muqdisho, *It.* Mogadiscio 55 D6

Mogilëv *see* Mahilyow

Mohéli *Island* Comoros 59 F2

Mohns Ridge *Undersea feature* Greenland Sea 63 F3

Mojave California, USA 25 C7

Mojave Desert *Desert* W USA 25 D7

Moldavia *see* Moldova

Molde Norway 65 A5

Moldova *Country* E Europe *var.* Moldavia 88

Molodechno *see* Maladzyechna

Molodeczno *see* Maladzyechna

Molotov *see* Perm'

Moluccas *see* Maluku

Molucca Sea *see* Maluku, Laut

Mombasa Kenya 55 D7

Monaco *Country* W Europe 71 E6

Monastir Tunisia 51 F1

Monclova Mexico 31 E2

Moncton Canada 19 F4

Mongo Chad 56 C3

Mongolia *Country* NE Asia 106-107

Monroe Louisiana, USA 28 B2

Monrovia *Capital of* Liberia 52 C5

Mons Belgium 67 B6

Montague Seamount *Undersea feature* Atlantic Ocean 43 H1

Montana *State* USA 22 C2

Montauban France 71 B6

Mont Blanc *Peak* France/Italy 60 D4

Mont-de-Marsan France 70 B6

Monte-Carlo Monaco 71 E6

Montecristi Dominican Republic 35 E3

Montego Bay Jamaica 34 C3

Montenegro *Republic* Yugoslavia 81 D5

Monterey California, USA 25 B6

Montería Colombia 38 B2

Montero Bolivia 40 D4

Monterrey Mexico 31 E2

Montes Claros Brazil 41 G4

Montevideo *Capital of* Uruguay 42 C5

Montgomery Alabama, USA 28 D3

Montpelier Vermont, USA 21 F2

Montpellier France 71 C6

Montréal Canada 19 E4

Montreux Switzerland 75 A5

Montserrat *External territory* UK, West Indies 35

Monument Valley *Valley* SW USA 26 C1

Monywa Myanmar 118 A3

Monza Italy 76 B2

Moora Australia 129 B6

Moorhead Minnesota, USA 23 E2

Moosonee Canada 18 C3

Mopti Mali 53 E3

Morava *River* C Europe 79 B6 80 E4

Moravská Ostrava *see* Ostrava

Morawhanna Guyana 39 F2

Moray Firth *Inlet* Scotland, UK 68 C3

Moree Australia 130 C2

Morehead City North Carolina, USA 29 G2

Morelia Mexico 31 E4

Morena, Sierra *Mountain range* Spain 72 D4

Morghāb *River* Afghanistan/Turkmenistan 102 D4

Morioka Japan 110 D3

Morocco *Country* N Africa 50

Morogoro Tanzania 55 C7

Morondava Madagascar 59 F3

Moroni *Capital of* Comoros 59 F2

Morotai, Pulau *Island* Indonesia 121 F3

Moscow *Capital of* Russian Federation *Rus.* Moskva 90 B4 94 B2

Mosel *River* W Europe *Fr.* Moselle 75 A5

Moselle *River* W Europe *Ger.* Mosel 67 E8 70 E4

Moshi Tanzania 55 C7

Moskva *see* Moscow

Mosquito Coast *Coastal region* Nicaragua 33 E3

Moss Norway 65 B6

Mossendjo Congo 57 B6

Mossoró Brazil 41 H2

Most Czech Republic *Ger.* Brüx 78 A4

Mostaganem Algeria 50 D1

Mostar Bosnia & Herzegovina 80 C4

Mosul *see* Al Mawşil

Motril Spain 73 E5

Moulins France 70 C4

Moulmein Myanmar 118 B4

Moundou Chad 56 C4

Mount Gambier Australia 130 A4

Mount Isa Australia 126 A5 130 A1

Mount Vernon Illinois, USA 20 B5

Mouscron Belgium 67 A6

Moyale Kenya 55 C5

Moyobamba Peru 40 B2

Mozambique *Country* SE Africa 59

Mozambique Channel *Sea Feature* Indian Ocean 59 F3

Mozambique Ridge *Undersea feature* Indian Ocean 49 D8

Mozyr' *see* Mazyr

Mpika Zambia 59 E2

Mtwara Tanzania 55 C8

Muang Khammouan Laos 118 D4

Muang Không Laos 119 D5

Muang Xaignabouri Laos 118 C3

Mufulira Zambia 58 D2

Mugla Turkey 96 A4

Mukacheve Ukraine 88 B2

Mulhacén *Peak* Spain 60 C5

Mulhouse France 70 E4

Mull *Island* Scotland, UK 68 B3

Muller, Pegunungan *Mountains* Indonesia 120 D4

Multān Pakistan 114 C2

Mumbai *see* Bombay

Muna, Pulau *Island* Indonesia 121 E4

München Germany *Eng.* Munich 75 C6

Muncie Indiana, USA 20 C4

Munich *see* München

Münster Germany 74 A4

Muonio *River* Finland/Sweden 64 D3

Muqdisho *see* Mogadishu

Mur *River* C Europe 75 D7

Murcia *Region* Spain 73 F4

Mures *River* Hungary/Romania 79 D7

Murfreesboro Tennessee, USA 28 D1

Murgab Tajikistan 103 F3

Murgab *River* Turkmenistan *var.* Murghab 102 C3

Murghab *see* Murgab

Müritz *Lake* Germany 74 D3

Murmansk Russian Federation 90 C2 94 C1

Murray *River* Australia 130 A3

Murrumbidgee *River* Australia 130 B3

Murska Sobota Slovenia 80 B2

Murzuq Libya 51 F3

Muş Turkey 97 F3

Muscat *Capital of* Oman *Ar.* Masqaţ 101 E5

Musgrave Ranges *Mountain range* Australia 129 D5

Mwanza Tanzania 55 B6

Mwene-Ditu Zaire 57 D7

Mweru, Lake *Lake* Zaire/Zambia 57 D7

Myanmar *Country* SE Asia *var.* Burma 118-119

Mykolayiv Ukraine *Rus.* Nikolayev 89 C4

Mysore India 116 D2

Mzuzu Malawi 59 E2

N

Naberezhnyye Chelny Russian Federation *prev.* Brezhnev 91 C5

Nacala Mozambique 59 F2

Næstved Denmark 65 D8

Naga Philippines 120 E1

Nagano Japan 110 C4

Nagasaki Japan 111 A6

Nāgercoil India 116 D3

Nagorno-Karabakh *Region* Azerbaijan 97 G2

Nagoya Japan 111 C5

Nāgpur India 114 D4

Nagqu China 106 C5

Nagykanizsa Hungary *Ger.* Grosskanizsa 79 C7

Nagyszombat *see* Trnava

Naha Japan 111 A8

Nain Canada 19 N2

Nairobi *Capital of* Kenya 55 C6

Najaf *see* An Najaf

Najrān Saudi Arabia 101 B6

Nakamura Japan 111 B6

Nakhichevan' *see* Naxçıvan

Nakhodka Russian Federation 94 C3

Nakhon Ratchasima Thailand 119 C5

Nakhon Sawan Thailand 119 C5

Nakhon Si Thammarat Thailand 119 C6

Nakina Canada 18 B3

Nakskov Denmark 65 D8

Nakuru Kenya 55 C6

Nal'chik Russian Federation 91 A7 94 A4

Namangan Uzbekistan 103 E2

Nam Đinh Vietnam 118 D3

Namib Desert *Desert* Namibia 58 B3

Namibe Angola 58 B2

Namibia *Country* southern Africa 58

Nampa Idaho, USA 24 D3

Namp'o North Korea 108 E4

Nampula Mozambique 59 F2

Namur Belgium 67 C6

Nanchang China 109 C6

Nancy France 70 D3

Nändad India 114 D5 116 D1

Nanjing China 109 D5

Nanning China 109 B7

Nanortalik Greenland 62 C4

Nantes France 70 B4

Napier New Zealand 131 H2

Naples *see* Napoli

Napo *River* Ecuador/Peru 40 B2

Napoli Italy *Eng.* Naples 77 D5

Narbonne France 71 C6

Nares Plain *Undersea feature* Atlantic Ocean 15 F4

Nares Strait *Sea feature* Canada/Greenland 62 A2

Narew *River* Poland 78 E3

Narmada *River* India 114 D4

Narsaq Greenland 62 C4

Narsaq Kujalleq Greenland 62 C4

Narva Estonia 86 E2

Narva *River* Estonia/Russian Federation 86 E2

Narva Bay *Sea feature* Gulf of Finland *Est.* Narva Laht, *Rus.* Narvskiy Zaliv 86 E2

Narva Laht *see* Narva Bay

Narvik Norway 64 C3

Narvskiy Zaliv *see* Narva Bay

Naryn Kyrgyzstan 103 G2

Naryn *River* Kyrgyzstan/Uzbekistan 103 F2

Nāshik India 114 C5

Nashville Tennessee, USA 28 D1

Nāsir, Buheiret *Reservoir* Egypt 55 B2

Nasiriya *see* An Nāşirīyah

Nassau *Capital of* Bahamas 34 C1

Natal Brazil 41 H3

Natitingou Benin 53 F4

Natuna, Kepulauan *Island group* Indonesia 120 C3

Nauru *Country* Pacific Ocean 126 D3

Navapolatsk Belarus *Rus.* Novopolotsk 87 D5

Navassa Island *External territory* USA, West Indies 34 D3

Navoi Uzbekistan *Uzb.* Nawoiy 102 D2

Nawābshāh Pakistan 114 B3

Nawoiy *see* Navoi

Naxçıvan Azerbaijan *Rus.* Nakhichevan' 97 G3

Náxos *Island* Greece 85 D6

Nazareth *see* Nazerat

Nazca Peru 40 B4

Nazerat Israel *Eng.* Nazareth 99 A5

Nazrēt Ethiopia 55 C5

Nazwá Oman 101 E5

N'Dalatando Angola 58 B1

Ndélé Central African Republic 56 C4

N'Djamena *Capital of* Chad 56 B3

Ndola Zambia 58 D2

Nebitdag Turkmenistan 102 B2

Nebraska *State* USA 22-23 E3

Neches *River* S USA 27 H3

Neckar *River* Germany 75 B6

Necochea Argentina 45 D5

Neftezavodsk *see* Seydi

Negēlē Ethiopia 55 C5

Negev *see* HaNegev

Negro, Río *River* Argentina 45 C5

Negro, Rio *River* Brazil/Uruguay 40 D2

Negro, Rio *River* N South America 38 D3

Negros *Island* Philippines 121 E2

Neiva Colombia 38 B3

Nellore India 117 E2

Nelson New Zealand 131 G3

Neman *River* NE Europe *Bel.* Nyoman, *Lith.* Nemunas, *Ger.* Memel, *Pol.* Niemen 86 B4

Nemunas *see* Neman

Nemuro Japan 110 E2

Nepal *Country* S Asia 115

Nepalganj Nepal 115 E3

Neretva *River* Bosnia & Herzegovina 80 C4

Neris *River* Belarus/Lithuania *Bel.* Vilıya, *Pol.* Wilja 86 C4

Ness, Loch *Lake* Scotland, UK 68 C3

Netherlands *Country* W Europe *var.* Holland 66-67

Netherlands Antilles *External territory* Netherlands, West Indies *prev.* Dutch West Indies 36 C1

Netze *see* Noteć

Neubrandenburg Germany 74 D3

Neuchâtel, Lac de *Lake* Switzerland 75 A7

Neuhäusl *see* Nové Zámky

Neumünster Germany 74 B2

Neuquén Argentina 45 C5

Neusiedler See *Lake* Austria/Hungary 75 E7

Neusohl *see* Banská Bystrica

Neutra *see* Nitra

Nevada *State* USA 24-25

Nevel' Russian Federation 90 A4

Nevers France 70 C4

Nevşehir Turkey 96 D3

New Amsterdam Guyana 39 G2

Newark New Jersey, USA 21 F3

New Britain *Island* Papua New Guinea 126 C3

New Brunswick *Province*
Canada 19 F4
New Caledonia *External territory*
France, Pacific Ocean 122 C4
Newcastle Australia 130 C3
Newcastle upon Tyne England,
UK 68 D4
New Delhi *Capital of* India
114 D3
Newfoundland *Province* Canada
19 G2
Newfoundland *Island* Canada
19 H3
Newfoundland Basin *Undersea
feature* Atlantic Ocean 46 B3
New Georgia *Island* Solomon Is
126 C3
New Guinea *Island* Pacific
Ocean 126 B3
New Hampshire *State* USA
21 G2
New Haven Connecticut, USA
21 G3
New Ireland *Island* Papua New
Guinea 126 C3
New Jersey *State* USA 21 F4
Newman Australia 128 B4
New Mexico *State* USA
26-27 D2
New Orleans Louisiana, USA
28 C3
New Plymouth New Zealand
131 G2
Newport Oregon, USA 24 A3
Newport News Virginia, USA
21 F5
New Providence *Island*
Bahamas 34 C1
Newry Northern Ireland, UK
69 B5
New Siberian Islands *see*
Novosibirskiye Ostrova
New Wales *State* Australia 130
B3
New York *State* USA 21 F3
New York New York, USA
21 F3
New Zealand *Country* Pacific
Ocean 131
Neyshābūr Iran 100 D3
Ngaoundéré Cameroon 56 B4
N'Giva Angola 58 B2
N'Guigmi Niger 53 H3
Nha Trang Vietnam 119 E5
Niagara Falls *Waterfall*
Canada/USA 18 D5 21 E3

Niamey *Capital of* Niger 53 F3
Niangay, Lac *Lake* Mali 52 E3
Nicaragua *Country* Central
America 32-33
Nicaragua, Lago de *Lake*
Nicaragua 32 D3
Nice France 71 E6
Nicobar Islands *Island group*
India 117 H3
Nicosia *Capital of* Cyprus
var. Lefkosia, *Turk.* Lefkoşa
96 C5
Nicoya, Golfo de *Sea feature*
Costa Rica 32 D4
Nicoya, Península de *Peninsula*
Costa Rica 32 D4
Niemen *see* Neman
Nieuw Amsterdam Suriname
39 H2
Niğde Turkey 96 D4
Niger *Country* W Africa 53
Niger *River* W Africa
52-53 D3
Niger Delta *Wetlands* Nigeria
48 B4
Nigeria *Country* W Africa 53
Niigata Japan 110 C4
Nijmegen Netherlands
66 D4
Nikolayev *see* Mykolayiv
Nikopol' Ukraine 89 F3
Nile *River* N Africa 54 B3
Nile Delta *Wetlands* Egypt
48 D2
Nîmes France 71 C6
Ninetyeast Ridge *Undersea
feature* Indian Ocean 112 C4
117 G5
Ningbo China 109 D6
Ningxia *Autonomous region*
China 108-109 B4
Nioro Mali 52 D3
Nipigon, Lake *Lake* Canada
18 B4
Niš Yugoslavia 80 E4
Nitra Slovakia *Ger.* Neutra,
Hung. Nyitra 79 C6
Nitra *River* Slovakia
Ger. Neutra, *Hung.* Nyitra
79 C6
Niue *External territory* New
Zealand, Pacific Ocean 122 D4
127 F4
Nizāmābād India 114 D5
116 D1

Nizhnevartovsk Russian
Federation 94 D3
Nizhniy Novgorod Russian
Federation *prev.* Gor'kiy
91 C5 94 B3
Nkhotakota Malawi 59 E2
Nkongsamba Cameroon 56 B4
Nordaustlandet *Island* Svalbard
63 H2
Norfolk Virginia, USA 21 F5
Norfolk *External territory*
Australia, Pacific Ocean
125 E3
Nori'lsk Russian Federation
94 D3
Norman Oklahoma, USA
26 F2
Normandie *Region* France
Eng. Normandy 70 B3
Normandy *see* Normandie
Normantown Australia 126 B4
Norrköping Sweden 65 C6
Norseman Australia 129 C6
North Albanian Alps *Mountains*
Albania/Yugoslavia 81 D5
North America 14-15
North American Basin *Undersea
feature* Atlantic Ocean 46 B4
North Andaman *Island* India
117 G2
North Atlantic Ocean 62-63
North Australian Basin *Undersea
feature* Indian Ocean 124 A2
128 A2
North Bay Canada 18 D4
North Cape *Coastal feature* New
Zealand 131 F1
North Cape *Coastal feature*
Norway 64 D2
North Carolina *State* USA 29 F1
North Dakota *State* USA
22-23 D2
Northern Cook Islands *Islands*
Cook Islands 127 G4
Northern Cyprus, Turkish
Republic of *Disputed region*
Cyprus 96 C5
Northern Dvina *River* Russian
Federation *see* Severnaya
Dvina 61 G2
Northern Ireland *Province* UK
68-69
Northern Marianas *External
territory* USA, Pacific Ocean
122 C2

Northern Sporades *see* Voreioi Sporades

Northern Territory *Territory* Australia 126 A4 128 E3

North European Plain *Region* N Europe 60-61 E3 92 B2

North Frisian Islands *Islands* Denmark/Germany 74 B2

North Island *Island* New Zealand 131 G2

North Korea *Country* E Asia 108

North Las Vegas Nevada, USA 25 D7

North Minch *Sea feature* Scotland, UK 68 C2

North Platte Nebraska, USA 23 E4

North Platte *River* C USA 22 D3

North Pole *Ice feature* Arctic Ocean 12 C4

North Sea Atlantic Ocean 68 E2

North Uist *Island* Scotland, UK 68 B3

North West Cape *Coastal feature* Australia 128 A4

Northwest Territories *Territory* Canada 17 F3

Norway *Country* N Europe 64-65

Norwegian Basin *Undersea feature* Atlantic Ocean 60 C1

Norwegian Sea Arctic Ocean 13 C8

Norwich England, UK 69 E6

Noteć *River* Poland *Ger.* Netze 78 C3

Nottingham England, UK 69 D6

Nottingham Island Hudson Strait 18 D1

Nouâdhibou Mauritania 52 B2

Nouâdhibou, Râs *Coastal feature* Mauritania 52 B2

Nouakchott *Capital of* Mauritania 52 B2

Nouméa *Capital of* New Caledonia 126 D5

Nova Gorica Slovenia 80 A2

Nova Gradiška Croatia 80 B3

Nova Iguaçu Brazil 41 F5 43 F2

Nova Kakhovka Ukraine 89 F4

Novara Italy 76 A2

Nova Scotia *Province* Canada 19 G4

Novaya Zemlya *Islands* Russian Federation 90 E2 94 D2

Nové Zámky Slovakia *Ger.* Neuhäusl, *Hung.* Érsekújvár 79 C6

Novgorod Russian Federation 90 B4 94 B2

Novi Sad Yugoslavia 80 D3

Novokuznetsk Russian Federation *prev.* Stalinsk 94 D4

Novo Mesto Slovenia 80 A2

Novopolotsk *see* Navapolatsk

Novosibirsk Russian Federation 94 D4

Novosibirskiye Ostrova *Islands* Russian Federation *Eng.* New Siberian Islands 12 D2 93 F1 95 F2

Novo Urgench *see* Urgench

Novyy Margilan *see* Fergana

Nsanje Malawi 59 E2

Nubian Desert *Desert* Sudan 54 B3

Nuevo Laredo Mexico 31 E2

Nuku'alofa *Capital of* Tonga 127 F5

Nukus Uzbekistan 102 C1

Nullarbor Plain *Region* Australia 129 D6

Nunivak Island *Island* Alaska, USA 16 B2

Nuoro Italy 77 A5

Nurek Tajikistan 103 E3

Nuremberg *see* Nürnberg

Nürnberg Germany *Eng.* Nuremberg 75 C6

Nuugaatsiaq Greenland 62 B3

Nuuk Greenland *var.* Godthåb 62 B4

Nyala Sudan 54 A4

Nyasa, Lake *Lake* E Africa 49 D5

Nyeboe Land *Region* Greenland 62 B2

Nyeri Kenya 55 C6

Nyíregyháza Hungary 79 E6

Nyitra *see* Nitra

Nykøbing-Falster Denmark 65 D8

Nyköping Sweden 65 C6

Nyoman *see* Neman

Nzérékoré Guinea 52 D4

O

Oakland California, USA 25 B6

Oakley Kansas, USA 23 E4

Oaxaca Mexico 31 F5

Ob' *River* Russian Federation 94 C3

Oban Scotland, UK 68 D3

Oberpahlen *see* Põltsamaa

Obihiro Japan 110 D2

Obo Central African Republic 56 D4

Oceania 124-125

Ocean Island *see* Banaba

Oceanside California, USA 25 C8

Ochamchira *see* Och'amch'ire

Och'amch'ire Georgia *Rus.* Ochamchira 97 E1

Oconee *River* SE USA 29 E3

Ödenburg *see* Sopron

Odense Denmark 65 D7

Oder *River* C Europe 74 F4 78 C4

Odesa Ukraine *Rus.* Odessa 89 E4

Odessa *see* Odesa

Odessa Texas, USA 27 E3

Odienné Ivory Coast 52 D4

Oesel *see* Saaremaa

Ofanto *River* Italy 77 D5

Offenbach Germany 75 B5

Ogaden *Plateau* Ethiopia 55 D5

Ogallala Nebraska, USA 22 D4

Ogbomosho Nigeria 53 F4

Ogden Utah, USA 22 B3

Ogdensburg New York, USA 21 F2

Oger *see* Ogre

Ogre Latvia *Ger.* Oger 86 C3

Ogulin Croatia 80 A3

Ohio *State* USA 20 D4

Ohio *River* N USA 20 B5

Ohrid Macedonia 81 D6

Ohrid, Lake *Lake* Albania/Macedonia 81 D6

Ohře *River* Czech Republic/Germany *Ger.* Eger 79 A5

Oil City Pennsylvania, USA 21 E3

Ōita Japan 111 B6

Oka *River* Russian Federation 95 E4

Okahandja Namibia 58 C3

Okavango *River var.* Cubango southern Africa 58 C2

Okavango Delta *Wetland* Botswana 58 C3

Okayama Japan 111 B5

Okazaki Japan 111 C5

Okeechobee, Lake *Lake* Florida, USA 29 F4

Okhotsk Russian Federation 95 G3

Okhotsk, Sea of Pacific Ocean 122 C1

Okinawa *Island* Japan 111 A8

Oki-shotō *Island group* Japan 111 B5

Oklahoma *State* USA 27 F1

Oklahoma City Oklahoma, USA 27 F2

Okushiri-tō *Island* Japan 110 C2

Okāra Pakistan 114 C2

Öland *Island* Sweden 65 C7

Olavarría Argentina 44 D4

Olbia Italy 77 A5

Oldenburg Germany 74 B3

Oleksandriya Ukraine *Rus.* Aleksandriya 89 E3

Oleněk Russian Federation 95 E3

Olhão Portugal 72 C5

Olita *see* Alytus

Olmaliq *see* Almalyk

Olmütz *see* Olomouc

Olomouc Czech Republic *Ger.* Olmütz 79 C5

Olsztyn Poland *Ger.* Allenstein 78 D2

Olt *River* Romania 88 B5

Olten Switzerland 75 B7

Olympia Washington, USA 24 B2

Omaha Nebraska, USA 23 F4

Oman *Country* SW Asia 101 D6

Oman, Gulf of *Sea feature* Indian Ocean 112 B2

Omdurman Sudan 54 B4

Omsk Russian Federation 94 C4

Ondangwa Namibia 58 C3

Onega *River* Russian Federation 90 B4

Onega, Lake *see* Onezhskoye Ozero

Onezhskoye Ozero *Lake* Russian Federation *Eng.* Lake Onega 90 B3

Ongole India 117 E2

Onitsha Nigeria 53 G5

Ontario *Province* Canada 18 B3

Ontario, Lake *Lake* Canada/USA 15 F3

Oostende Belgium *Eng.* Ostend 67 A5

Oosterschelde *Inlet* Netherlands 66 B4

Opole Poland *Ger.* Oppeln 78 C4

Oporto *see* Porto

Oppeln *see* Opole

Oradea Romania 88 B3

Oran Algeria 50 D1

Orange Australia 130 C3

Orange River *River* southern Africa 58 C4

Oranjestad Netherlands Antilles 35 E5

Ord *River* Australia 128 D3

Ordu Turkey 96 D2

Ordzhonikidze *see* Vladikavkaz

Örebro Sweden 65 C6

Oregon *State* USA 24

Orël Russian Federation 81 A5

Orem Utah, USA 22 B4

Orenburg Russian Federation 91 C6 94 B4

Orense *see* Ourense

Orestiáda Greece 84 D3

Orhon *River* Mongolia 107 E2

Orinoco *River* Colombia/Venezuela 39 E3

Orissa *State* India 115 E5

Oristano Italy 77 A5

Orizaba, Pico de *see* Citlaltépetl

Orkney *Islands* Scotland, UK 68 C2

Orlando Florida, USA 29 E4

Orléans France 70 C4

Ormsö *see* Vormsi

Örnsköldsvik Sweden 65 C5

Orontes *River* SW Asia 98 B3

Orosirá Rodópis *see* Rhodope Mountains

Orsha Belarus 87 E5

Orsk Russian Federation 91 D6 94 B4

Oruro Bolivia 40 C4

Ōsaka Japan 111 C5

Ösel *see* Saaremaa

Osh Kyrgyzstan 103 F2

Oshawa Canada 18 D5

Oshkosh Wisconsin, USA 20 B2

Osijek Croatia 80 C3

Oslo *Capital of* Norway 65 B6

Osmaniye Turkey 96 D4

Osnabrück Germany 74 B4

Osorno Chile 45 B5

Oss Netherlands 66 D4

Ossora Russian Federation 95 H2

Ostend *see* Oostende

Östersund Sweden 65 C5

Ostfriesische Inseln *Islands* Germany *Eng.* East Frisian Islands 74 A3

Ostrava Czech Republic *Ger.* Mährisch-Ostrau, *prev.* Moravská Ostrava 79 C5

Ostrołęka Poland 78 D3

Ostrowiec Świętokrzyski Poland 78 D4

Ōsumi-shotō *Island group* Japan 111 A7

Otaru Japan 110 D2

Otra *River* Norway 65 A6

Otranto Italy 77 E5

Otranto, Strait of *Sea feature* Albania/Italy 81 C6

Ottawa *Capital of* Canada 18 D5

Ottawa *River* Canada 18 D4

Ou *River* Laos 118 C3

Ouachita *River* SE USA 28 B2

Ouagadougou *Capital of* Burkina 53 E4

Ouahigouya Burkina 53 E3

Ouargla Algeria 51 E2

Oudtshoorn South Africa 58 C5

Ouémé *River* Benin 53 F4

Ouessant, Île d' *Island* France 70 A3

Ouésso Congo 57 C5

Oujda Morocco 50 D2

Oulu Finland 64 D4

Oulu *River* Finland 64 D4

Oulujärvi *Lake* Finland 64 E4

Ounas *River* Finland 64 D3

Pechora *River* Russian Federation 90 D3

Pecos Texas, USA 27 E3

Pecos *River* SW USA 26 D2

Pécs Hungary *Ger.* Fünfkirchen 79 C7

Pegu Myanmar 118 B4

Peipsi Järv *see* Peipus, Lake

Peipus, Lake *Lake* Estonia/Russian Federation *Est.* Peipsi Järv, *Rus.* Chudskoye Ozero 86 D2

Peiraías Greece *var.* Piraiévs, *Eng.* Piraeus 83 F3 85 C5

Peking *see* Beijing

Pelagie, Isola *Island* Italy 77 B8

Peloponnese *see* Pelopónnisos

Pelopónnisos *Peninsula* Greece *Eng.* Peloponnese 85 B6

Pelotas Brazil 42 C4

Pelotas *River* Brazil 42 D3

Pematangsiantar Indonesia 120 A3

Pemba *Island* Tanzania 49 E5

Pendleton Oregon, USA 24 C2

Pennines *Hills* England, UK 68 D4

Pennsylvania *State* USA 20-21

Penong Australia 129 D6

Penonomé Panama 33 F5

Pensacola Florida, USA 28 D3

Penza Russian Federation 91 B5

Penzance England, UK 69 C7

Peoria Illinois, USA 20 B4

Pereira Colombia 38 B3

Périgueux France 71 B5

Perm' Russian Federation *prev.* Molotov 91 D5 94 B3

Pernau *see* Pärnu

Pernik Bulgaria *prev.* Dimitrovo 84 B2

Pernov *see* Pärnu

Perpignan France 71 C6

Persian Gulf *see feature* Arabian Sea *var.* The Gulf 112 B2

Perth Australia 129 B6

Perth Scotland, UK 68 C3

Perth Basin *Undersea feature* Indian Ocean 124 A3

Peru C South America 40

Peru Basin *Undersea feature* Pacific Ocean 123 G4

Peru-Chile Trench *Undersea feature* Pacific Ocean 123 G4

Perugia Italy 76 C4

Pescara Italy 76 D4

Peshāwar Pakistan 114 C1

Petaḥ Tiqwa Israel 99 A5

Peterborough England, UK 69 E6

Peterborough Canada 18 D5

Peter the First Island *Island* Antarctica 132 A4

Petra Jordan 99 B6

Petrich Bulgaria 84 B3

Petroaleksandrovsk *see* Turtkul'

Petrograd *see* St Petersburg

Petropavlovsk Russian Federation 94 C4

Petropavlovsk-Kamchatskiy Russian Federation 95 H3

Petrozavodsk Russian Federation 90 B3

Pevek Russian Federation 95 G1

Pforzheim Germany 75 B6

Phangan, Ko *Island* Thailand 119 C6

Philadelphia Pennsylvania, USA 21 F4

Philippines *Country* Asia 121

Philippine Sea Pacific Ocean 121 F1

Philippopolis *see* Plovdiv

Phnom Penh *Capital of* Cambodia 119 D6

Phoenix Arizona, USA 26 B2

Phoenix Islands *Island group* Kiribati 127 F3

Phôngsali Laos 118 C3

Phuket Thailand 119 B7

Phuket, Ko *Island* Thailand 119 B7

Phumĭ Sâmraô ng Cambodia 119 D5

Piacenza Italy 76 B2

Pianosa *Island* Italy 76 D4

Piatra-Neamţ Romania 88 C3

Piave *River* Italy 76 C2

Pielinen *Lake* Finland 64 E4

Pierre South Dakota, USA 23 E3

Piešťany Slovakia *Ger.* Pistyan, *Hung.* Pöstyén 79 C6

Pietermaritzburg South Africa 58 D4

Pihkva Järv *see* Pskov, Lake

Piła Poland *Ger.* Schneidemühl 78 C3

Pilar Paraguay 42 B3

Pilchilemu Chile 44 B4

Pilcomayo *River* C South America 42 B2 44 D2

Pillau *see* Baltiysk

Pilsen *see* Plzeň

Pinang, Pulau *Island* Malaysia 120 B3

Pinar del Río Cuba 34 A2

Píndos *Mountain range* Greece *Eng.* Pindus Mountains 61 E5 84 A4

Pindus Mountains *see* Pindos

Pine Bluff Arkansas, USA 28 B2

Pinega *River* Russian Federation 90 C3

Pineiós *River* Greece 84 B4

Pine Island Bay *Sea feature* Antarctica 132 B3

Ping, Mae Nam *River* Thailand 118 C4

Pingxiang China 109 B7

Pínnes, Ákra *Coastal feature* Greece 84 C4

Pinsk Belarus *Pol.* Pińsk 87 B4

Piraeus *see* Peiraías

Piraiévs *see* Peiraías

Pisa Italy 76 B3

Pisco Peru 40 B4

Pishpek *see* Bishkek

Pistyan *see* Piešťany

Pitcairn Islands *External territory* UK, Pacific Ocean 123 E4

Piteå Sweden 64 D4

Piteşti Romania 88 C4

Pittsburgh Pennsylvania, USA 21 E4

Pituffik Greenland 62 A2

Piura Peru 40 A2

Pivdennyy Bug *River* Ukraine 89 E3

Plasencia Spain 72 D3

Plate *River* Argentina/Uruguay 42 B5 44 D4

Platte *River* C USA 23 E4

Plattensee *see* Balaton

Plenty, Bay of *Sea feature* New Zealand 131 H2

Pleven Bulgaria 84 C1

Płock Poland 78 D3

Prome Myanmar 118 A4

Prossnitz *see* Prostějov

Prostějov Czech Republic
Ger. Prossnitz 79 C5

Provence *Region* France 71 D6

Providence Rhode Island, USA
21 G3

Providencia, Isla de *Island*
Colombia 33 E3 34 B4

Provo Utah, USA 22 B4

Prudhoe Bay Alaska, USA
16 D2

Prydz Bay *Sea feature* Antarctica
133 G2

Przheval'sk *see* Karakol

Pskov Russian Federation 90 A4

Pskov, Lake *Lake*
Estonia/Russian Federation
Est. Pihkva Järv,
Rus. Pskovskoye Ozero 86 D3

Pskovskoye Ozero *see* Pskov,
Lake

Ptich' *see* Ptsich

Ptsich *River* Belarus
Rus. Ptich' 87 D6

Pucallpa Peru 40 B3

Puebla Mexico 31 F4

Puerto Aisén Chile 45 B6

Puerto Bahía Negra Paraguay
42 F3

Puerto Barrios Guatemala 32 C2

Puerto Busch Bolivia 40 D5

Puerto Carreño Colombia 38 D2

Puerto Cortés Honduras 32 C2

Puerto Deseado Argentina
45 C7

Puerto Maldonado Peru 40 C4

Puerto Montt Chile 45 B5

Puerto Natales Chile 45 B7

Puerto Plata Dominican
Republic 35 E3

Puerto Princesa Philippines
120 E2

Puerto Rico *External territory*
USA, West Indies 35 F3

Puerto Rico Trench *Undersea
feature* Caribbean Sea 35 F3

Puerto Santa Cruz Argentina
45 C7

Puerto Suárez Bolivia 40 D5

Puerto Vallarta Mexico 30 D4

Puerto Williams Chile 45 C8

Pula Croatia 80 B2

Punakha Bhutan 115 G3

Punata Bolivia 40 C4

Pune India *prev.* Poona 114 C5
116 C1

Punjab *State* India 114 C2

Puno Peru 40 C4

Punta Arenas Chile
prev. Magallanes 45 B8

Puntarenas Costa Rica 32 D4

Purmerend Netherlands 66 C3

Purus *River* Brazil/Peru 40 C3

Pusan South Korea 108 E4

Putumayo *River* NW South
America 38 C4

Pyandzh *see* Panj

Pyapon Myanmar 118 B4

Pyarnu *see* Pärnu

Pyinmana Myanmar 118 B3

Pyongyang *Capital of* North
Korea 108 E4

Pyramiden Svalbard 63 G2

Pyramid Lake *Lake* Nevada,
USA 25 C5

Pyrenees *Mountain range* SW
Europe 60 C5

Q

Qaanaaq Greenland *var.* Thule
62 A2

Qal'eh-ye Now Afghanistan
102 D4

Qamdo China 106 D5

Qandahār *see* Kandahār

Qaqortoq Greenland 62 C4

Qara Qum *see* Karakumy

Qarshi *see* Karshi

Qasigiannguit Greenland 62 B3

Qatar *Country* SW Asia 101 D5

Qattara Depression *see* Qaṭṭāra,
Monkhafad el

Qaṭṭāra, Monkhafad el *Desert
basin* Egypt *Eng.* Qattara
Depression 48 C2 54 A1

Qena Egypt 54 B2

Qeqertarsuaq Greenland 62 B3

Qeqertarsuaq *Island* Greenland
62 B3

Qeqertarsuatsiaat Greenland
62 B4

Qilian Shan *Mountain range*
China 106 D4

Qingdao China 108 D4

Qinghai Hu *Lake* China *var.*
Koko Nor 106 D4

Qing-Zang Gaoyuan *Plateau*
China *Eng.* Plateau of Tibet
104 C2 106 B4

Qin Ling *Mountains* China
109 B5

Qiqihar China 108 D3

Qizilqum *see* Kyzyl Kum

Qom Iran *var.* Kum 100 C3

Qondūz *River* Afghanistan
103 E4

Qondūz *see* Kunduz

Quba Azerbaijan *Rus.* Kuba
97 H2

Québec Canada 19 E4

Québec *Province* Canada 18 D3

Queen Charlotte Islands *Islands*
Canada 16 D5

Queen Charlotte Sound *Sea
feature* Canada 16 D5

Queen Elizabeth Islands *Islands*
Canada 17 F1

Queen Maud Land *Region*
Antarctica 133 E1

Queensland *State* Australia 126
B5 130 B5

Queenstown New Zealand
131 F4

Quelimane Mozambique 59 E4

Querétaro Mexico 31 E4

Quetta Pakistan 114 B2

Quezaltenango Guatemala
32 B2

Quibdó Colombia 38 B2

Quimper France 70 A3

Qui Nhon Vietnam 119 E5

Quito *Capital of* Ecuador 38 A4

Qüqon *see* Kokand

Qyteti Stalin *see* Kuçovë

R

Raab *see* Győr

Raab *see* Rába

Rába *River* Austria/Hungary
Ger. Raab 79 C7

Rabat *Capital of* Morocco 50 C2

Race, Cape *Coastal feature*
Canada 15 G3 19 H4

Rach Gia Vietnam 119 D6

Radom Poland 78 D4

Radviliškis Lithuania 86 B4

Ragusa Italy 77 D7

Rahīmyār Khān Pakistan 114 C3

Rainier, Mount Peak USA 14 D3

Raipur India 115 E5

Rājahmundry India 117 E1

Rajang River Malaysia 120 D3

Rājasthān State India 114 C3

Rājkot India 114 C4

Rājshāhi Bangladesh 115 G4

Rakvere Estonia Ger. Wesenberg 86 D2

Raleigh North Carolina, USA 29 F1

Ralik Chain Islands Marshall Islands 126 D1

Râmnicu Vâlcea Romania prev. Rîmnicu Vîlcea 88 B4

Ramree Island Island Myanmar 118 A3

Rancagua Chile 44 B4

Rānchi India 115 F4

Randers Denmark 65 A7

Rangoon Capital of Myanmar Bur. Yangon 118 B4

Rankin Inlet Canada 17 G3

Rankumara Range Mountain range New Zealand 131 H2

Rapid City South Dakota, USA 22 D3

Rarotonga Island Cook Islands 127 G5

Rasht Iran 100 C3

Ratak Chain Islands Marshall Islands 126 D1

Ratchaburi Thailand 119 C5

Rauma Finland 65 D5

Ravenna Italy 76 C3

Rāwalpindi Pakistan 114 C1

Rawson Argentina 45 C6

Razgrad Bulgaria 84 D1

Reading England, UK 69 D7

Rebun-tō Island Japan 110 C1

Rechytsa Belarus 87 D7

Recife Brazil 41 H3

Red Deer Canada 17 E5

Redding California, USA 25 B5

Red River River S USA 27 G2 28 B3

Red River River China/Vietnam 118 D3

Red Sea Indian Ocean 112 A3

Regensburg Germany 75 C6

Reggane Algeria 50 D3

Reggio di Calabria Italy 77 D7

Reggio nell' Emilia Italy 76 B3

Regina Canada 17 F5

Rehoboth Namibia 58 C3

Reichenberg see Liberec

Reims France Eng. Rheims 70 D3

Reindeer Lake Lake Canada 15 E2

Reni Ukraine 88 D4

Rennes France 70 B3

Reno Nevada, USA 25 B5

Resistencia Argentina 44 D3

Reşiţa Romania 88 B4

Resolute Canada 17 F2

Réunion External territory France, Indian Ocean 113 B5

Reus Spain 73 G2

Reval see Tallinn

Revel see Tallinn

Revillagigedo, Islas Island Mexico 30 C4

Rey, Isla del Island Panama 33 F5

Reykjavík Capital of Iceland 63 E4

Reynosa Mexico 31 E2

Rēzekne Latvia Ger. Rositten, Rus. Rezhitsa 86 D4

Rezhitsa see Rēzekne

Rheims see Reims

Rhine River W Europe 60 D4

Rhode Island State USA 21 G3

Rhodes see Ródos

Rhodope Mountains Mountain range Bulgaria/Greece Gk. Orosirá Rodópis, Bul. Despoto Planina 84 C3

Rhondda Wales, UK 69 C6

Rhône River France/Switzerland 60 C4

Ribeirão Preto Brazil 41 F5 43 E1

Riberalta Bolivia 40 C3

Rîbniţa Moldova 88 D3

Richland Washington, USA 24 C2

Richmond Virginia, USA 21 E5

Riga Capital of Latvia Latv. Rīga 86 C3

Riga, Gulf of Sea feature Baltic Sea 86 C3

Riihimäki Finland 65 D5

Riiser-Larsen Ice Shelf Ice feature Antarctica 132 D1

Rijeka Croatia It. Fiume 80 A3

Rimini Italy 76 C3

Rîmnicu Vîlcea see Râmnicu Vâlcea

Riobamba Ecuador 38 A4

Rio Branco Brazil 40 C3

Río Cuarto Argentina 44 C4

Rio de Janeiro Brazil 41 G5 43 F2

Río Gallegos Argentina 45 C7

Rio Grande R N America 14 D4

Rio Grande Rise Undersea feature Atlantic Ocean 47 C6

Río Negro, Embalse del Reservoir Uruguay 42 C5

Rishiri-tō Island Japan 110 C1

Rivas Nicaragua 32 D3

Rivera Uruguay 42 C4

Riverside California, USA 25 C8

Rivne Ukraine Rus. Rovno 88 C2

Riyadh Capital of Saudi Arabia Ar. Ar Riyāḍ 101 C5

Rize Turkey 97 E2

Rkîz, Lac Lake Mauritania 52 B3

Road Town Capital of British Virgin Islands 35 F3

Roanne France 71 D5

Roanoke Virginia, USA 21 E5

Roanoke River SE USA 29 G1

Rochester Minnesota, USA 23 F3

Rochester New York, USA 21 E3

Rockall Island UK 46 C2

Rockhampton Australia 126 B5 130 C1

Rockingham Australia 129 B6

Rock Island Illinois, USA 20 A3

Rock Springs Wyoming, USA 22 C3

Rockstone Guyana 39 G2

Rocky Mountains Mountain range Canada/USA 16-17 22

Rodez France 71 C6

Ródhos see Ródos

Ródos Island Greece var. Ródhos, Eng. Rhodes 83 F3 85 E6

Ródos Greece *Eng.* Rhodes
85 E6
Rodosto *see* Tekirdağ
Roeselare Belgium 67 A6
Roma Australia 130 C2
Roma *see* Rome
Romania *Country* SE Europe 88
Romanovka Russian Federation
95 F4
Rome *Capital of* Italy *It.* Roma
76 C4
Rome Georgia, USA 28 D2
Rønne Denmark 65 D8
Rønne Ice Shelf *Ice feature*
Antarctica 132 C2
Roosendaal Netherlands 66 C4
Rosario Argentina 44 D4
Roseau *Capital of* Dominica
35 G4
Rosenau *see* Rožňava
Rositten *see* Rēzekne
Ross Dependency *Territory* New
Zealand, Antarctica 132-133
Ross Ice Shelf *Ice feature*
Antarctica 132 D4
Rosso Mauritania 52 B3
Ross Sea Antarctica 132 D5
Rostak *see* Ar Rustāq
Rostock Germany 74 C2
Rostov-na-Donu Russian
Federation 91 A6 94 A3
Roswell New Mexico, USA
26 D2
Rotorua New Zealand 131 G2
Rotterdam Netherlands 66 C4
Rouen France 70 C3
Rovaniemi Finland 64 D3
Rovno *see* Rivne
Rovuma *River* Mozambique/
Tanzania 55 B7 59 F2
Rožňava Slovakia *Ger.* Rosenau,
Hung. Rozsnyó 79 D6
Rozsnyó *see* Rožňava
Rub' al Khali *Desert* SW Asia
Eng. Great Sandy Desert,
Empty Quarter 101 D6
Rudnyy Kazakhstan 94 B4
Rudolf, Lake *Lake* Ethiopia/
Kenya *var.* Lake Turkana
48 D4 55 D5
Ruiz *Peak* Colombia 36 B2
Rumbek Sudan 55 B5
Rundu Namibia 58 C3

Ruse Bulgaria 84 D1
Russian Federation *Country*
Europe/Asia 90-91 94-95
Rust'avi Georgia 97 G2
Rutland Vermont, USA 21 F2
Rwanda *Country* C Africa 55
Ryazan' Russian Federation 91
B5 94 B3
Rybach'ye *see* Issyk-Kul'
Rybinskoye Vodokhranilishche
Reservoir Russian Federation
Eng. Rybinsk Reservoir 90 B4
Rybnik Poland 79 C5
Ryūkyū-rettō *Island group* Japan
111 A8
Rzeszów Poland 79 E5

S

Saale *River* Germany 74 C4
Saarbrücken Germany 75 A6
Saare *see* Saaremaa
Saaremaa *Island* Estonia
var. Saare, Sarema, *Ger.* Ösel,
var. Oesel 86 C2
Sabadell Spain 73 G2
Sabhā Libya 51 F3
Sable, Cape *Coastal feature*
Canada 19 F5
Sabzevār Iran 100 D3
Sacramento California, USA
25 B6
Şa'dah Yemen 101 B6
Sado *Island* Japan 110 C4
Safi Morocco 50 B2
Saginaw Michigan, USA 20 C3
Sahara *Desert* N Africa 48 B3
Sahel *Region* W Africa 48 B3
53 F3
Saïda Lebanon *anc.* Sidon 98 B4
Saidpur Bangladesh 115 G3
Saigon *see* Hồ Chí Minh
Saimaa *Lake* Finland 65 E5
Saint-Brieuc France 70 A3
Saint Catherines Canada 18 D5
Saint-Chamond France 71 D5
St Christopher & Nevis *see* St
Kitts & Nevis
St Cloud Minnesota, USA 23 F2
St-Denis *Capital of* Réunion
59 H3

Saintes France 70 B5
Saint-Étienne France 71 D5
St. George's *Capital of* Grenada
35 G5
St Helena *External territory* UK,
Atlantic Ocean 47 D5
St Helens, Mount *Peak* USA
14 D3
St Helier *Capital* Jersey 69 D8
Saint-Jean, Lake *Lake* Canada
19 E4
Saint John Canada 19 F4
Saint John's Canada 19 H3
St Joseph Missouri, USA 23 F4
St Kitts & Nevis *Country* West
Indies *var.* St Christopher &
Nevis 35
St.-Laurent-du-Maroni French
Guiana 39 H2
Saint Lawrence *River* Canada
19 E4
Saint Lawrence, Gulf of *Sea
feature* Canada 19 G4
St. Lawrence Island *Island*
Alaska, USA 16 B2
Saint-Lô France 71 B3
Saint-Louis Senegal 52 B3
St Louis Missouri, USA 23 G4
St Lucia *Country* West Indies 35
Saint-Malo France 70 B3
Saint-Nazaire France 70 A4
St Paul Minnesota, USA 23 F2
St Peter Port *Capital of* Guernsey
69 D8
St Petersburg Russian
Federation *Rus.* Sankt-
Peterburg, *prev.* Leningrad,
Petrograd 90 B3 94 B2
St Petersburg Florida, USA
29 E4
St Pierre Canada 19 H4
Saint Pierre Saint Pierre &
Miquelon 19 H4
Saint Pierre & Miquelon
External territory France,
Atlantic Ocean 19 H4
St Vincent, Cape *see* São Vicente,
Cabo de
St Vincent & The Grenadines
Country West Indies 35
Sajama *Peak* Bolivia 36 B4
Sakākah Saudi Arabia 100 B4
Sakakawea, Lake *Lake* North
Dakota, USA 22 D2

Sakarya *see* Adapazarı
Sakhalin *Island* Russian Federation 95 H4
Salado *River* Argentina 44 C3
Şalālah Oman 101 D6
Salamanca Spain 72 D2
Sala y Gómez *Island* Chile, Pacific Ocean 123 F4
Saldus Latvia *Ger.* Frauenburg 86 B3
Sale Australia 130 B4
Salekhard Russian Federation 94 D3
Salem India 116 D2
Salem Oregon, USA 24 B3
Salerno Italy 77 D5
Salerno, Golfo di *Sea feature* Italy 77 D5
Salihorsk Belarus *Rus.* Soligorsk 87 C6
Salima Malawi 59 E2
Salina *Island* Italy 77 D6
Salina Utah, USA 22 B4
Salinas California, USA 25 B6
Salinas Grandes *Lowpoint* Argentina 44 C3
Salisbury England, UK 69 D7
Salisbury Island Canada 18 D1
Salonica *see* Thessaloníki
Salso *River* Italy 77 C7
Salt *see* As Salt
Salta Argentina 44 C2
Saltillo Mexico 31 E2
Salt Lake City Utah, USA 22 B2
Salto Uruguay 42 B4
Salton Sea *Lake* California, USA 25 D8
Salvador Brazil 41 H4
Salween *River* SE Asia 104 C3
Salzburg Austria 75 D7
Salzgitter Germany 74 C4
Samaná Dominican Republic 35 E3
Samar *Island* Philippines 121 F2
Samara Russian Federation 91 C6 H4 B3
Samarinda Indonesia 120 D4
Samarkand Uzbekistan 102 D2
Sambre *River* Belgium 67 B7
Samobor Croatia 80 B2
Sámos *Island* Greece 85 D5

Samothrace *see* Samothráki
Samothráki *Island* Greece *Eng.* Samothrace 84 D3
Samsun Turkey 96 D2
Samui, Ko *Island group* Thailand 119 C6
San *River* Cambodia/Vietnam 118-119
San *River* Poland 79 E5
Saña Peru 40 A3
Sana *Capital* of Yemen *var.* Şan'ā' 101 B7
San Ambrosio, Isla *Island* Chile 44 A3
San Andrés, Isla de *Island* Colombia 33 E3 34 B5
San Angelo Texas, USA 27 F3
San Antonio Chile 44 B4
San Antonio Texas, USA 27 F4
San Antonio *River* S USA 27 G4
San Antonio Oeste Argentina 45 C5
Sanāw Yemen 101 C6
San Bernardino California, USA 25 C7
San Carlos Uruguay 42 C5
San Carlos de Bariloche Argentina 45 B5
San Clemente Island *Island* W USA 25 C8
San Cristóbal Venezuela 38 C2
San Diego California, USA 25 C8
San Félix, Isla *Island* Chile 44 A2
San Fernando Chile 44 B4
San Fernando Trinidad & Tobago 35 G5
San Fernando Venezuela 38 D2
San Francisco California, USA 25 B6
San Ignacio Belize 32 C1
San Ignacio Paraguay 42 B3
San Joaquin *River* W USA 25 B6
San Jorge, Golfo *Sea feature* Argentina 37 C6
San José *Capital* of Costa Rica 32 D4
San Jose California, USA 25 B6
San José del Guaviare Colombia 38 C3
San Juan Argentina 44 B3
San Juan *River* Costa Rica/Nicaragua 32 D4

San Juan *Capital* of Puerto Rico 35 F3
San Juan de los Morros Venezuela 38 D1
Sankt Gallen Switzerland 75 B7
Sankt Martin *see* Martin
Sankt-Peterburg *see* St Petersburg
Sankt Pölten Austria 75 E6
Şanlıurfa Turkey *prev.* Urfa 96 E4
San Lorenzo Honduras 32 C3
San Luis Potosí Mexico 31 E3
San Marino *Country* S Europe 76 C3
San Matías, Golfo *Sea feature* Argentina 37 C6
San Miguel El Salvador 32 C3
San Miguel de Tucumán Argentina 44 C3
San Nicolas Island *Island* W USA 25 C8
San Pedro Sula Honduras 32 C2
San Remo Italy 76 A3
San Salvador *Capital* of El Salvador 32 C3
San Salvador de Jujuy Argentina 44 C2
San Sebastián Spain *Bas.* Donostia 73 E1
Santa Ana El Salvador 32 B2
Santa Ana California, USA 25 C8
Santa Barbara California, USA 25 B7
Santa Catalina Island *Island* W USA 25 C8
Santa Clara Cuba 34 B2
Santa Cruz Bolivia 40 D4
Santa Cruz California, USA 25 B6
Santa Cruz Islands *Island group* Solomon Islands 126 D3
Santa Fe Argentina 44 D3
Santa Fe New Mexico, USA 26 D2
Santa Maria Brazil 42 C4
Santa Marta Colombia 38 C1
Santander Spain 73 E1
Santanilla, Islas *Islands* Honduras 33 E1
Santarém Brazil 41 E2
Santarém Portugal 72 C3

Santa Rosa Argentina 45 C4
Santa Rosa California, USA 25 A6
Santa Rosa de Copán Honduras 32 C2
Santa Rosa Island Island W USA 25 B8
Santee River SE USA 29 F2
Santiago Capital of Chile 44 B4
Santiago Dominican Republic 35 E3
Santiago Panama 33 F5
Santiago Spain 72 C1
Santiago de Cuba Cuba 34 C3
Santiago del Estero Argentina 44 C3
Santo Domingo Capital of Dominican Republic 35 E3
Santo Domingo de los Colorados Ecuador 38 A4
Santos Brazil 43 E2
Santos Plateau Undersea feature Atlantic Ocean 43 E3
Sanya China 109 B8
São Borja Brazil 42 C3
São Francisco River Brazil 41 G3
São José do Rio Preto Brazil 42 D1
São Luís Brazil 41 G2
Saône River France 70 D4
São Paulo Brazil 41 F5 43 E2
São Roque, Cabo de Coastal feature Brazil 36 E3
São Tomé Capital of Sao Tome & Principe 57 A5
São Tomé Island Sao Tome & Principe 57 A6
Sao Tome & Principe Country W Africa 57
São Vicente, Cabo de Coastal feature Portugal Eng. Cape St Vincent 60 B5 72 B5
Sapporo Japan 110 D2
Saragossa see Zaragoza
Sarajevo Capital of Bosnia & Herzegovina 80 C4
Sarandë Albania 81 D7
Saransk Russian Federation 91 B5
Saratov Russian Federation 91 B6
Sarawak State Malaysia 120 D3

Sardegna Island Italy Eng. Sardinia 77 B5 83 D3
Sardinia see Sardegna
Sarema see Saaremaa
Sargasso Sea Atlantic Ocean 46 B4
Sargodha Pakistan 114 C2
Sarh Chad 56 C4
Saruhan see Manisa
Sasebo Japan 111 A6
Saskatchewan Province Canada 17 F5
Saskatchewan River Canada 17 F5
Saskatoon Canada 17 F5
Sassari Italy 77 A5
Satu Mare Romania 88 B3
Saudi Arabia Country SW Asia 100-101
Sault Sainte Marie Canada 18 C4
Sault Sainte Marie Michigan, USA 20 C1
Saurimo Angola 58 C1
Sava River SE Europe 80 C3
Savannah Georgia, USA 29 F3
Savannah River SE USA 29 E2
Savannakhét Laos 118 D4
Savissivik Greenland 62 A2
Savona Italy 76 A3
Savonlinna Finland 65 E5
Şawqirah Oman 101 D6
Sayat Turkmenistan 102 D3
Sayhūt Yemen 101 D6
Saynshand Mongolia 107 E2
Say 'ün Yemen 101 C6
Schaffhausen Switzerland 75 B7
Schaulen see Šiauliai
Schefferville Canada 19 E2
Scheldt River W Europe 67 B5
Schiermonnikoog Island Netherlands 66 D1
Schneidemühl see Piła
Schwäbische Alb Mountains Germany 75 B6
Schwarzwald Forested mountain region Germany Eng. Black Forest 75 B6
Schwerin Germany 74 C3
Schweriner See Lake Germany 74 C3
Scilly, Isles of Islands UK 69 B8

Scotia Ridge Undersea feature Atlantic Ocean 47 B7
Scotia Sea Atlantic Ocean 47 B7
Scotland National region UK 68
Scottsbluff Nebraska, USA 22 D3
Scottsdale Arizona, USA 26 B2
Scranton Pennsylvania, USA 21 F3
Scutari, Lake Lake Albania/Yugoslavia 81 C5
Seattle Washington, USA 24 B2
Ségou Mali 52 D3
Segovia Spain 73 E2
Segura River Spain 73 E4
Seikan Tunnel Tunnel Japan 110 D3
Seinäjoki Finland 65 D5
Seine River France 70 C3
Sekondi-Takoradi Ghana 53 E5
Selfoss Iceland 63 E4
Selma Alabama, USA 28 D3
Semara Western Sahara 50 B3
Semarang Indonesia 120 C5
Semipalatinsk Kazakhstan 94 D4
Sên River Cambodia 118-119 D5
Sendai Japan 110 D4
Senegal Country W Africa 52
Senegal River Africa 52 B3
Seoul Capital of South Korea Kor. Sŏul 108 E4
Sept-Iles Canada 19 F3
Seraing Belgium 67 D6
Seram Island Indonesia 121 F4
Serbia Republic Yugoslavia 80 D3
Seremban Malaysia 120 B3
Sermersuaq Region Greenland 62 B2
Serov Russian Federation 94 C3
Serpent's Mouth, The Sea feature Trinidad & Tobago/Venezuela Sp. Boca de la Serpiente 39 F1
Serra do Mar Mountains Brazil 42 D3
Sérres Greece 84 C3
Sétif Algeria 51 E1
Setúbal Portugal 72 C4
Seul, Lake Lake Canada 18 A3
Sevana Lich Lake Armenia 97 G2
Sevastopol' Ukraine 89 C5

Skellefteå Sweden 64 D4

Skopje *Capital of* Macedonia 81 E5

Skövde Sweden 65 B6

Skovorodino Russian Federation 95 F4

Skye *Island* Scotland, UK 68 B3

Slavonski Brod Croatia 80 C3

Sligo Ireland 69 A5

Sliven Bulgaria 84 D2

Slonim Belarus 87 B6

Slovakia *Country* C Europe 79

Slovenia *Country* SE Europe 80

Slov'yans'k Ukraine 89 G5

Słupsk Poland *Ger.* Stolp 78 C2

Slutsk Belarus 87 C6

Smallwood Reservoir *Lake* Canada 19 E3

Smederevo Yugoslavia 80 D3

Smolensk Russian Federation 90 A4

Smyrna *see* İzmir

Snake *River* NW USA 24 D4

Snowdonia *Mountains* Wales, UK 69 C6

Sobradinho, Represa de *Reservoir* Brazil 41 G3

Sochi Russian Federation 91 A7 94 A3

Société, Îles de la *Islands* French Polynesia *Eng.* Society Islands 125 H3 127 H4

Society Islands *see* Société, Îles de la

Socotra *see* Suquţrá

Sodankylä Finland 64 D3

Sofia *Capital of* Bulgaria *var.* Sofija, *Bul.* Sofiya 84 C2

Sofija *see* Sofia

Sofiya *see* Sofia

Sognefjorden *Inlet* Norway 65 A5

Sohâg Egypt 54 B2

Sohm Plain *Undersea feature* Atlantic Ocean 15 F4 19 H5

Sokhumi Georgia *Rus.* Sukhumi 97 E1

Sokodé Togo 53 F4

Sokoto Nigeria 53 F3

Sokoto *River* Nigeria 53 G3

Solāpur India 114 D5 116 D1

Soligorsk *see* Salihorsk

Solomon Islands *Country* Pacific Ocean 126

Solomon Sea Pacific Ocean 126 C3

Somalia *Country* E Africa 54-55

Somali Basin *Undersea feature* Indian Ocean 112 B3

Sombor Yugoslavia 80 C2

Somerset Island *Island* Canada 17 F2

Somme *River* France 70 C3

Somoto Nicaragua 32 D3

Songea Tanzania 55 C8

Songkhla Thailand 119 C7

Sonoran Desert *Desert* Mexico/USA 26 A2

Sopron Hungary *Ger.* Ödenburg 79 B6

Soria Spain 73 E2

Sorocaba Brazil 41 F5 43 E2

Sorrento Italy 77 D5

Sosnowiec Poland *Ger.* Sosnowitz 79 C5

Sosnowitz *see* Sosnowiec

Soûr Lebanon *anc.* Tyre 98 A4

Sousse Tunisia 51 F1

South Africa *Country* southern Africa 58-59

South America 36-37

Southampton England, UK 69 D7

Southampton Island *Island* Canada 15 F2

South Andaman *Island* India 117 G2

South Atlantic Ocean 47 C7

South Australia *State* Australia 129 E5 130 A2

South Australian Basin *Undersea feature* Southern Ocean 124 B5 129 C7

South Bend Indiana, USA 20 C3

South Carolina *State* USA 29 F2

South Carpathians *see* Carpaţii Meridionali

South China Sea Pacific Ocean 122 B2

South Dakota *State* USA 22-23 D2

South East Cape *Coastal feature* Australia 130 B5

Southeast Indian Ridge *Undersea feature* Indian Ocean 113 E6

Southeast Pacific Basin *Undersea feature* Pacific Ocean 123 F5

Southend-on-Sea England, UK 69 E6

Southern Alps *Mountain range* New Zealand 131 E4

Southern Cook Islands *Islands* Cook Islands 127 G5

Southern Upland *Mountain range* Scotland, UK 68 C4

South Fiji Basin *Undersea feature* Pacific Ocean 125 E3

South Georgia *External territory* UK, Atlantic Ocean 37 E7

South Indian Basin *Undersea feature* Indian Ocean 113 E7

South Island *Island* New Zealand 131 F4

South Korea *Country* E Asia 108-109

South Orkney Islands *Islands* Antarctica 37 D8

South Polar Plateau *Upland* Antarctica 132 D3

South Pole *Ice feature* Antarctica 132 D3

South Sandwich Islands *External territory* UK, Atlantic Ocean 37 E8

South Shetland Islands *Islands* Antarctica 47 B7

South Uist *Island* UK 68 B3

Southwest Indian Ridge *Undersea feature* Indian Ocean 113 B6

Southwest Pacific Basin *Undersea feature* Pacific Ocean 133 G5

Sovetsk Kaliningrad, Russian Federation *prev.* Tilsit 86 B4

Soweto South Africa 58 D4

Spain *Country* SW Europe 72-73

Sparks Nevada, USA 25 C5

Sparta *see* Spárti

Spartanburg South Carolina, USA 29 E2

Spárti Greece *Eng.* Sparta 85 B6

Spitsbergen *Island* Svalbard 63 G2

Split Croatia 80 B4

Spokane Washington, USA 24 C2

Spratly Islands *Islands* South China Sea 120 D2

Syrian Desert

Springfield Illinois, USA
20 B4
Springfield Massachusetts, USA
21 G3
Springfield Missouri, USA
23 F5
Springfield Oregon, USA 24 B3
Srebrenica Bosnia &
Herzegovina 80 C4
Sri Lanka *Country* S Asia
prev. Ceylon 117
Srīnagar India 114 D1
Srīnagarind Reservoir *Reservoir*
Thailand 119 C5
Stalinabad *see* Dushanbe
Stalingrad *see* Volgograd
Stalin Peak *see* Communism
Peak
Stalinsk *see* Novokuznetsk
Stambul *see* Istanbul
Stanleyville *see* Kisangani
Stanovoy Range *Mountain range*
Russian Federation 93 F3
Stara Planina *see* Balkan
Mountains
Stara Zagora Bulgaria 84 D2
Stavanger Norway 65 A6
Stavropol' Russian Federation
91 A7 94 A3
Steinamanger *see* Szombathely
Steinkjer Norway 64 B4
Stepanakert *see* Xankändi
Stettin *see* Szczecin
Stewart Island *Island* New
Zealand 131 F5
Štip Macedonia 81 E5
Stirling Scotland, UK 68 C4
Stockerau Austria 75 E6
Stockholm *Capital* of Sweden
65 C6
Stockton California, USA 25 B6
Stœng Treng Cambodia 119 D5
Stoke-on-Trent England, UK
69 D6
Stolp *see* Słupsk
Stornoway Scotland, UK 68 B2
Stralsund Germany 74 D2
Stranraer Scotland, UK 68 C4
Strasbourg France
Ger. Strassburg 70 E4
Stratford-upon-Avon England,
UK 69 D6
Stratonice Czech Republic 79 A5

Strimon *see* Struma
Stromboli *Island* Italy 77 D6
Struma *prev.* Ceylon
Bulgaria/Greece *Gk.* Strimon,
var. Strymon 84 C3
Strumica Macedonia 81 E5
Strymon *see* Struma
Stuhlweissenburg *see*
Székesfehérvár
Stuttgart Germany 75 B6
Subotica Yugoslavia 80 D2
Suceava Romania 88 C3
Sucre *Capital* of Bolivia 40 C5
Sudan *Region* NE Africa 54-55
Sudbury Canada 18 C4
Sudd *Region* Sudan 55 B5
Sudeten *Mountains* Central
Europe *var.* Sudetes, Sudetic
Mountains, *Cz./Pol.* Sudety
79 B5
Sudetes *see* Sudeten
Sudetic Mountains *see* Sudeten
Sudety *see* Sudeten
Suez Egypt 54 B1
Suez, Gulf of *Sea feature* Red Sea
99 A8
Suez Canal *Canal* Egypt
Ar. Qanāt as Suways 48 D2
Şuhār Oman 101 D5
Sühbaatar Mongolia 107 E1
Sukhumi *see* Sokhumi
Sukkur Pakistan 114 B3
Sula, Kepulauan *Island group*
Indonesia 121 F4
Sulawesi *Island* Indonesia
Eng. Celebes 121 E4
Sulu Archipelago *Island group*
Philippines 121 E3
Sülüktü *see* Sulyukta
Sulu Sea Pacific Ocean 121 E2
Sulyukta Kyrgyzstan
Kir. Sülüktü 103 E2
Sumatra *Island* Indonesia 121 B4
Sumba *Island* Indonesia 121 E5
Sumbawanga Tanzania 55 B7
Sumbe Angola 58 B2
Sumgait *see* Sumqayıt
Sumqayıt Azerbaijan
Rus. Sumgait 97 H2
Sumy Ukraine 89 F2
Sunderland England, UK 68 D4
Sundsvall Sweden 65 C5
Suntar Russian Federation 94 F3

Sunyani Ghana 53 E4
Superior Wisconsin, USA 20 A1
Superior, Lake *Lake*
Canada/USA 15 E3
Suquţrá *Island* Yemen
var. Socotra 101 D7 112 B3
Şūr Oman 101 E5
Surabaya Indonesia 120 D5
Sūrat India 114 C5
Surat Thani Thailand 119 C6
Sûre *River* W Europe 67 D7
Surigao Philippines 120 F2
Surinam *see* Suriname 39
Suriname *Country* NE South
America *var.* Surinam 39
Surkhob *River* Tajikistan 103 E3
Surt Libya *var.* Sidra 51 G2
Surt, Khalīj *Sea feature*
Mediterranean Sea *Eng.* Gulf
of Sirte, Gulf of Sidra 51 G2
83 E4
Susanville California, USA
25 B5
Suways, Qanât as *see* Suez Canal
Suva *Capital* of Fiji 127 E4
Svalbard *External territory*
Norway, Arctic Ocean 63 G2
Svay Riêng Cambodia 119 D6
Sverdlovsk *see* Yekaterinburg
Svetlogorsk *see* Svyetlahorsk
Svyetlahorsk Belarus
Rus. Svetlogorsk 87 D7
Swakopmund Namibia 58 B3
Swansea Wales, UK 69 C6
Swaziland *Country* southern
Africa 58-59
Sweden *Country* N Europe
64-65
Sweetwater Texas, USA 27 F3
Swindon England, UK 69 D6
Switzerland *Country*
C Europe 75
Sydney Australia 130 C3
Sydney Canada 19 G4
Syktyvkar Russian Federation
90 D4 94 C3
Sylhet Bangladesh 115 G4
Syracuse *see* Siracusa
Syracuse New York, USA 21 F3
Syr Darya *River* C Asia 92 C3
Syria *Country* SW Asia 98-99
Syrian Desert *Desert* SW Asia
Ar. Bādiyat ash Shām 100 A3

183

Szczecin Poland *Ger.* Stettin 78 B3

Szeged Hungary *Ger.* Szegedin 79 D7

Szegedin *see* Szeged

Székesfehérvár Hungary *Ger.* Stuhlweissenburg 79 C7

Szekszárd Hungary 79 C7

Szolnok Hungary 79 D7

Szombathely Hungary *Ger.* Steinamanger 79 B7

T

Tabariya, Bahrat *see* Tiberius, Lake

Tábor Czech Republic 79 B5

Tabora Tanzania 55 B7

Tabrīz Iran 100 C2

Tabuaeran *Island* Kiribati 127 G2

Tabūk Saudi Arabia 100 A4

Tacloban Philippines 120 F2

Tacna Peru 40 C4

Tacoma Washington, USA 24 B2

Tacuarembó Uruguay 42 C4

Tadmur *see* Tudmur

Taegu South Korea 108 E4

Taejŏn South Korea 108 E4

Taguatinga Brazil 41 F4

Tagus *River* Portugal/Spain *Port.* Tejo, *Sp.* Tajo 72 C3

Tahiti *Island* French Polynesia 12 7H4

Tahoe, Lake *Lake* W USA 25 B5

Taipei *Capital* of Taiwan 109 D6

Taiping Malaysia 120 B3

Taiwan *Country* E Asia *prev.* Formosa 109

Taiwan Strait *Sea feature* East China Sea/South China Sea *var.* Formosa Strait 109 D7

Taiyuan China 108 C4

Ta'izz Yemen 101 B7

Tajikistan *Country* C Asia 103

Tajo *see* Tagus

Takla Makan *see* Taklimakan Shamo

Taklimakan Shamo *Desert region* China *var.* Takla Makan 104 B2 106 B3

Talamanca, Cordillera de *Mountains* Costa Rica 33 E4

Talas Kyrgyzstan 103 F2

Talaud, Kepulauan *Island group* Indonesia 121 F3

Talca Chile 44 B4

Talcahuano Chile 44 B4

Taldy-Kurgan Kazakhstan 94 C5

Tallahassee Florida, USA 28 D3

Tallinn *Capital* of Estonia *prev.* Revel, *Ger.* Reval, *Rus.* Tallin 86 D2

Talsen *see* Talsi

Talsi Latvia *Ger.* Talsen 86 B3

Tamale Ghana 53 E4

Tamanrasset Algeria 51 E4

Tambov Russian Federation 91 B5

Tamil Nādu *State* India 116 C2

Tampa Florida, USA 29 E4

Tampere Finland 65 D5

Tampico Mexico 31 F3

Tamworth Australia 130 C3

Tana *River* Finland/Norway 64 D2

Tanami Desert *Desert* Australia 128 D4

Tananarive *see* Antananarivo

Tanega-shima *Island* Japan 111 B7

Tanga Tanzania 55 C7

Tanganyika, Lake *Lake* E Africa 49 D5

Tanger Morocco *var.* Tangiers 50 C1

Tanggula Shan *Mountain range* China 106 C4

Tangiers *see* Tanger

Tangra Yumco *Lake* China 106 B5

Tangshan China 108 D4

Tanimbar Islands *see* Tanimbar, Kepulauan

Tanimbar, Kepulauan *Island group* Indonesia *Eng.* Tanimbar Islands 121 G5

Tanjungkarang Indonesia 120 B5

Tantā Egypt 54 B1

Tan-Tan Morocco 50 B3

Tanzania *Country* E Africa 55

Taos New Mexico, USA 26 D1

Tapa Estonia *Ger.* Taps 86 D2

Tapachula Mexico 31 G5

Tapajós *River* Brazil 41 E2

Tāpi *River* India 114 C4

Taps *see* Tapa

Ṭarābulus *see* Tripoli, Lebanon

Ṭarābulus al-Gharb *see* Tripoli, Libya

Taranto Italy 77 E5

Taranto, Golfo di *Sea feature* Mediterranean Sea 77 E5

Tarapoto Peru 40 B2

Tarawa *Island* Kiribati 127 E2

Tarbes France 71 B6

Tarcoola Australia 129 E6

Târgoviște Romania *prev.* Tîrgoviște 88 C4

Târgu Mureș Romania *prev.* Tîrgu Mureș 88 C4

Tarija Bolivia 40 C5

Tarim He *River* China 106 B3

Tarn *River* France 71 C6

Tarnów Poland 79 D5

Tarragona Spain 73 G2

Tarsus Turkey 96 D4

Tartu Estonia *prev.* Yur'yev, *var.* Yurev, *Ger.* Dorpat 86 D3

Ṭarṭūs Syria 98 B3

Tashauz *see* Dashkhovuz

Tashkent *Capital* of Uzbekistan *var.* Taškent, *Uzb.* Toshkent 103 E2

Tasiusaq Greenland 62 B3

Tasmania *State* Australia 130 B5

Tasman Plateau *Undersea feature* Pacific Ocean 124 D5

Tasman Sea *Pacific* Ocean 122 C4

Tassili N'Ajjer *Desert plateau* Algeria 51 E4

Tatabánya Hungary 79 C6

Tatar Pazardzhik *see* Pazardzhik

Taubaté Brazil 41 F5 43 E2

Taunggyi Myanmar 118 B3

Taunton England, UK 69 C7

Taupo New Zealand 131 G2

Taupo, Lake *Lake* New Zealand 131 G2

Tauragė Lithuania 86 B4

Tauranga New Zealand 131 H2

Taurus Mountains *Mountain range* Turkey *see* Toros Dağları 92 D4

Tavoy Myanmar 119 B5

Tawau Malaysia 120 D3

Taymyr, Ozero *Lake* Russian
Federation 95 E2
Taymyr, Poluostrov *Peninsula*
Russian Federation *Eng.*
Taymyr Peninsula 93 E1 95 E2
Taymyr Peninsula *see* Taymyr,
Poluostrov
Tbilisi *Capital of* Georgia
Geor. T'bilisi, *prev.* Tiflis 97 F2
Tedzhen Turkmenistan
Turkm. Tejen 102 C3
Tegucigalpa *Capital of* Honduras
32 C2
Teheran *see* Tehrān
Tehrān *Capital of* Iran
prev. Teheran 100 C3
Tehuantepec, Golfo de *Sea
feature* Mexico 31 G5
Tejen *see* Tedzhen
Tejo *see* Tagus
Tekirdağ Turkey *It.* Rodosto
96 A2
Tel Aviv-Yafo Israel 99 A5
Teles Pires *River* Brazil 41 E3
Tell Atlas *Plateau* Africa 82 C3
Tel'man *see* Tel'mansk
Tel'mansk Turkmenistan
Turkm. Tel'man 102 C2
Telschen *see* Telšiai
Telšiai Lithuania *Ger.* Telschen
86 B3
Temuco Chile 45 B5
Tenerife *Island* Spain 50 A3
Tennant Creek Australia 126 A5
128 E3
Tennessee *State* USA 28 D1
Tennessee *River* SE USA 29 C1
Tepelenë Albania 81 D6
Tepic Mexico 30 D4
Teplice Czech Republic *Ger.*
Teplitz, *prev.* Teplice-Šanov,
Ger. Teplitz-Schönau 78 A4
Teplice-Šanov *see* Teplice
Teplitz *see* Teplice
Teplitz-Schönau *see* Teplice
Teraina *Island* Kiribati 127 G2
Teresina Brazil 41 G2
Termez Uzbekistan 103 E3
Terneuzen Netherlands 67 B5
Terni Italy 76 C4
Ternopil' Ukraine
Rus. Ternopol' 88 C2
Terrassa Spain 73 G2

Terschelling *Island* Netherlands
66 C1
Teruel Spain 73 F3
Teseney Eritrea 54 C4
Tete Mozambique 59 E2
Tétouan Morocco 50 C1
Tetovo Macedonia 81 D5
Tetschen *see* Děčín
Tevere *River* Italy 76 C4
Texas *State* USA 26-27
Texas City Texas, USA 27 G4
Texel *Island* Netherlands 66 C2
Thailand *Country* SE Asia
118-119
Thailand, Gulf of *Sea feature*
South China Sea 119 C6
Thames *River* England, UK
69 D6
Thāne India 115 C5 116 C1
Thar Desert *Desert*
India/Pakistan 114 C3
Thásos *Island* Greece 84 C3
Thaton Myanmar 118 B4
Theiss *see* Tisza
Thermaic Gulf *see* Thermaïkós
Kólpos
Thermaïkós Kólpos *Sea feature*
Greece *Eng.* Thermaic Gulf
84 B4
Thessaloníki Greece
var. Salonica 84 B3
Thiès Senegal 52 B3
Thiladunmathi Atoll *Island*
Maldives 116 C4
Thimphu *Capital of* Bhutan
115 G3
Thionville France 70 D3
Thíra *Island* Greece 85 D6
Thompson Canada 17 G4
Thon Buri Thailand 119 C5
Thorn *see* Toruń
Thorshavn *see* Tórshavn
Thracian Sea Greece
Gk. Thrakikó Pélagos 84 D3
Thrakikó Pélagos *see* Thracian
Sea
Thule *see* Qaanaaq
Thun Switzerland 75 A7
Thunder Bay Canada 18 B4
Thüringer Wald *Forested moun-
tains* Germany 75 C5
Thurso Scotland, UK 68 C2
Tianjin China *var.* Tientsin
108 D4

Tiaret Algeria 50 D1
Tiberias, Lake Israel
var. Sea of Galilee, *Heb.* Yam
Kinneret, *Ar.* Bahrat Tabariya
99 B5
Tibesti *Mountains* Chad/Libya
48 C3
Tibet *Autonomous region* China
Chin. Xizang 106 C3
Tibet, Plateau of *see* Qing-Zang
Gaoyuan
Tienen Belgium 67 C6
Tien Shan *Mountain range*
C Asia 92 D4
Tientsin *see* Tianjin
Tierra del Fuego *Island*
Argentina/Chile 45 C8
Tiflis *see* Tbilisi
Tighina Moldova *prev.* Bendery
88 D4
Tigris *River* SW Asia 92 B4
Tijuana Mexico 30 A1
Tiksi Russian Federation 95 F2
Tilburg Netherlands 66 C4
Tillabéri Niger 53 F3
Tilsit *see* Sovetsk
Timaru New Zealand 131 F4
Timişoara Romania 88 A4
Timmins Canada 18 C4
Timor *Island* Indonesia 121 F5
Timor Sea Indian Ocean
112 E4
Timor Trough *Undersea feature*
Indian Ocean 128 C1
Tindouf Algeria 50 B3
Tínos *Island* Greece 85 D5
Tirana *Capital of* Albania 81 D6
Tiraspol Moldova 88 A4
Tîrgoviște *see* Târgoviște
Tîrgu Mureș *see* Târgu Mureș
Tirol *Region* Austria *var.* Tyrol
75 C7
Tirso *River* Italy 77 A5
Tiruchchirāppalli India 116 D3
Tisa *see* Tisza
Tisza *River* E Europe *Ger.*
Theiss, *Cz./Rom./SCr.* Tisa
79 D6
Titicaca, Lake *Lake* Bolivia/Peru
40 C4
Titov Veles Macedonia 81 E5
Tlemcen Algeria 50 D2
Toamasina Madagascar 59 G3

Toba, Danau *Lake* Indonesia 120 A3

Toba Kākar Range *Mountains* Pakistan 114 B2

Tobruk *see* Ṭubruq

Tocantins *River* Brazil 41 E3

Tocopilla Chile 44 B2

Togo *Country* W Africa 53 F4

Tokat Turkey 96 D3

Tokelau *External territory* New Zealand, Pacific Ocean 123

Tokmak Kyrgyzstan 103 F2

Tokuno-shima *Island* Japan 111 A8

Tokushima Japan 111 B5

Tokyo *Capital of* Japan 111 D5

Toledo Spain 73 E3

Toledo Ohio, USA 20 D3

Toledo Bend Reservoir *Reservoir* S USA 27 H3

Toliara Madagascar 59 F3

Tol'yatti *prev.* Stavropol' Russian Federation 91 C5

Tomakomai Japan 110 D2

Tombouctou Mali 53 E3

Tombua Angola 58 B2

Tomini, Teluk *Sea feature* Indonesia 121 E4

Tomsk Russian Federation 94 D4

Tomur Feng *see* Pobedy

Tonga *Country* Pacific Ocean 122

Tongking, Gulf of *Sea feature* South China Sea *var.* Gulf of Tonkin 109 B7 118 E3

Tongliao China 107 G2

Tongtian He *River* China 106 C4

Tonkin, Gulf of *see* Tongking, Gulf of

Tônlé Sap *Lake* Cambodia 119 D5

Tonopah Nevada, USA 25 C5

Toowoomba Australia 130 C2

Topeka Kansas, USA 23 F4

Torino Italy *Eng.* Turin 76 A2

Tori-shima *Island* Japan 111 D6

Torkestān, Band-e *Mountain range* Afghanistan 102 D4

Torneälv *River* Sweden 64 D3

Tornio Finland 64 D4

Tornio *River* Finland/Sweden 64 D3

Toronto Canada 18 D5

Toros Dağları *Mountain range* Turkey *Eng.* Taurus Mountains 96 C4

Torrens, Lake *Lake* Australia 130 A2

Torreón Mexico 30 D2

Torres Strait *Sea feature* Arafura Sea/Coral Sea 126 B4

Torrington Wyoming, USA 22 D3

Tórshavn *Capital of* Faeroe Islands *Dan.* Thorshavn 63 F4

Tortoise Islands *see* Galapagos Islands

Tortosa Spain 73 F3

Toruń Poland *Ger.* Thorn 78 C3

Toscana *Region* Italy *Eng.* Tuscany 76 B3

Toscano, Arcipelago *Island group* Italy 76 B4

Toshkent *see* Tashkent

Tottori Japan 111 B5

Toubkal *Peak* Morocco 48 A2

Touggourt Algeria 51 E2

Toulon France 71 D6

Toulouse France 71 B6

Toungoo Myanmar 118 B4

Tournai Belgium 67 B6

Tours France 70 B4

Townsville Australia 126 B5

Towuti, Danau *Lake* Indonesia 121 E4

Toyama Japan 110 C4

Tozeur Tunisia 51 E2

Trâblous *see* Tripoli, Lebanon

Trabzon Turkey *Eng.* Trebizond 97 E2

Tralee Ireland 69 A6

Trang Thailand 119 C7

Transantarctic Mountains *Mountain range* Antarctica 132 D3

Transylvania *Region* Romania 88 B3

Transylvanian Alps *see* Carpaţii Meridionali

Trapani Italy 77 C6

Traun Austria 75 D6

Traunsee *Lake* Austria 75 D7

Traverse City Michigan, USA 20 C2

Travis, Lake *Lake* Texas, USA 27 F3

Trebinje Bosnia & Herzegovina 81 C5

Trebizond *see* Trabzon

Trelew Argentina 45 C6

Tremiti, Isole *Island group* Italy 76 D4

Trenčín Slovakia *Ger.* Trentschin *Hung.* Trencsén 79 C6

Trencsén *see* Trenčín

Trento Italy *Ger.* Trient 76 C2

Trenton New Jersey, USA 21 F4

Trentschin *see* Trenčín

Tres Arroyos Argentina 45 D5

Treviso Italy 76 C2

Trient *see* Trento

Trier Germany 75 A5

Trieste Italy 76 D2

Tríkala Greece 84 B4

Trincomalee Sri Lanka 117 E3

Trindade *External territory* Brazil, Atlantic Ocean 47 C6

Trinidad Bolivia 40 C4

Trinidad Uruguay 42 B5

Trinidad *Island* Trinidad & Tobago 36 C1

Trinidad & Tobago *Country* West Indies 35 H5

Trípoli Greece 85 B6

Tripoli Lebanon *var.* Trâblous, Ţarābulus 98 B3

Tripoli *Capital of* Libya *Ar.* Ţarābulus al-Gharb 51 F2

Tristan da Cunha *External territory* UK, Atlantic Ocean 47 D6

Trivandrum India 116 D3

Trnava Slovakia *Ger.* Tyrnau, *Hung.* Nagyszombat 79 C6

Trois-Rivières Canada 19 E4

Trollhättan Sweden 65 B6

Tromsø Norway 64 C2

Trondheim Norway 64 B4

Trondheimsfjorden *Inlet* Norway 64 A4

Troyes France 70 D4

Trujillo Honduras 32 D2

Trujillo Peru 40 A3

Tsarigrad *see* İstanbul

Tschenstochau *see* Częstochowa

Tselinograd *see* Akmola

Tsetserleg Mongolia 106 D2

Victoria Island *Island* Canada 17 F2

Victoria Land *Region* Antarctica 133 E5

Victoria Nyanza *see* Victoria, Lake

Vidin Bulgaria 84 B1

Viedma Argentina 45 C5

Viekšniai Lithuania 86 B3

Vienna *Capital of* Austria *Ger.* Wien 75 E6

Vientiane *Capital of* Laos 118 C4

Vietnam *Country* SE Asia 118-119

Vigo Spain 72 C2

Vijayawāda India 117 E1

Vila Nova de Gaia Portugal 72 C2

Vila Real Portugal 72 C2

Viliya *see* Neris

Viljandi Estonia *Ger.* Fellin 86 D2

Villach Austria 75 D7

Villahermosa Mexico 31 G4

Villarrica *Peak* Chile 37 B6

Villavicencio Colombia 38 C3

Vilna *see* Vilnius

Vilnius *Capital of* Lithuania *Pol.* Wilno, *Ger.* Wilna, *Rus.* Vilna 87 C5

Viña del Mar Chile 44 B4

Vinh Vietnam 118 D4

Vinnitsa *see* Vinnytsya

Vinnytsya Ukraine *Rus.* Vinnitsa 88 D2

Vinson Massif *Peak* Antarctica 132 B3

Virgin Islands *External territory* USA, West Indies 35 F3

Virginia Minnesota, USA 23 F2

Virginia *State* USA 20-21

Virovitica Croatia 80 B2

Virtsu Estonia *Ger.* Werder 86 C2

Visākhapatnam India 115 E5 117 E1

Visalia California, USA 25 C7

Visby Sweden 65 C7

Viscount Melville Sound *Sea feature* Arctic Ocean 17 F2

Viseu Portugal 72 C3

Vistula *see* Wisła

Vitebsk *see* Vitsyebsk

Viterbo Italy 76 C4

Viti Levu *Island* Fiji 125 F2 127 E4

Vitória Brazil 41 G5 43 G1

Vitoria Spain 73 E1

Vitória da Conquista Brazil 41 G4

Vitória Seamount *Undersea feature* Atlantic Ocean 43 G1

Vitsyebsk Belarus *Rus.* Vitebsk 86 E5

Vjosës, Lumi i *River* Albania 81 D6

Vladikavkaz Russian Federation *prev.* Ordzhonikidze, Dzaudzhikau 91 A7

Vladimir Russian Federation 91 B5

Vladimirovka *see* Yuzhno-Sakhalinsk

Vladivostok Russian Federation 95 G5

Vlieland *Island* Netherlands 66 C1

Vlissingen Netherlands *Eng.* Flushing 67 B5

Vlorë Albania 81 D6

Vojvodina *Region* Yugoslavia 80 D3

Volga *River* Russian Federation 94 A3

Volga Delta *Wetland* Russian Federation 61 G4

Volgograd Russian Federation *prev.* Stalingrad 91 B6 94 A3

Volkovysk *see* Vawkavysk

Vologda Russian Federation 90 B4 94 B2

Vólos Greece 84 B4

Volta, Lake *Lake* Ghana 53 E4

Volta Redonda Brazil 43 E2

Voreioi Sporades *Island group* Greece *Eng.* Northern Sporades 84 C4

Vorkuta Russian Federation 90 E3 94 D2

Vormsi *Island* Estonia *Ger.* Worms, *Swed.* Ormsö 86 C2

Voronezh Russian Federation 91 B5

Võrtsjärv *Lake* Estonia 86 D3

Võru Estonia *Ger.* Werro 86 D3

Vosges *Mountain range* France 70 E4

Vostochno-Sibirskoye More Arctic Ocean *Eng.* East Siberian Sea 12 D2 95 G1

Vostok Island *Island* Kiribati 127 H3

Vrangel'ya, Ostrov *Island* Russian Federation *Eng.* Wrangel Island 12 C1 95 G1

Vratsa Bulgaria 84 C2

Vršac Yugoslavia 80 D3

Vukovar Croatia 80 C3

Vulcano *Island* Italy 77 D6

Vyatka *River* Russian Federation 91 C5

W

Wa Ghana 53 E4

Waag *see* Váh

Waal *River* Netherlands 66 D4

Wabash *River* C USA 20 B4

Waco Texas, USA 27 G3

Waddeneilanden *Island group* Netherlands *Eng.* West Frisian Islands 66 C1

Waddenzee *Sea feature* Netherlands 66 D1

Wadi Halfa Sudan 54 B3

Wad Medani Sudan 54 B4

Wagga Wagga Australia 130 B3

Wagin Australia 129 B6

Waigeo, Pulau *Island* Indonesia 121 G4

Wakayama Japan 111 C5

Wakkanai Japan 110 D1

Wałbrzych Poland *Ger.* Waldenburg 78 B4

Waldenburg *see* Wałbrzych

Wales *National region* UK *Wel.* Cymru 69

Walk *see* Valga

Walla Walla Washington, USA 24 C2

Wallis & Futuna *External territory* France, Pacific Ocean 122 D3

Walvis Bay Namibia 58 B3

Walvis Ridge *Undersea feature* Atlantic Ocean 47 D6

Wandel Sea Arctic Ocean 63 E1

Wanganui New Zealand 131 G3

Wanlaweyn Somalia 55 B6

MAP FINDER

NORTH & WEST ASIA 92

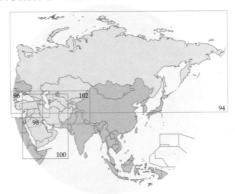

EAST & SOUTH ASIA 104

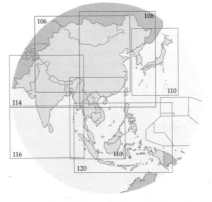